Traumatic Experiences of Nurses

Traumatic Experiences of Nurses
When your Profession Becomes a Nightmare

Huub Buyssen

Translated by Sylvia Dierks-Mallett

Jessica Kingsley Publishers
London and Bristol, Pennsylvania

Table 1.2 reproduced by kind permission of Nursing Times.

Table 1.5 and the checklists in Part 2, Chapter 2 reproduced by kind permission of Bradford City Council.

First published in the Netherlands in 1994 by De Tijdstroom

First published in the United Kingdom in 1996 by
Jessica Kingsley Publishers Ltd
116 Pentonville Road
London N1 9JB, England
and
1900 Frost Road, Suite 101
Bristol, PA 19007, U S A

Copyright © 1996 Huub Buyssen

Translator Sylvia Dierks-Mallett

Library of Congress Cataloging in Publication Data
Buyssen, Huub
Traumatic experiences of nurses : when your profession
becomes a nightmare
1. Nurses – Job stress 2. Nursing 3. Psychic trauma
I. Title
610.7'3'069

British Library Cataloguing in Publication Data
Buyssen, Huub
Traumatic Experiences of Nurses
When Your Profession Becomes a Nightmare
I. Title
616.8521

ISBN 1-85302-377-9

Printed and Bound in Great Britain by
Biddles Ltd, Guildford and King's Lynn

Contents

This book is dedicated to the nurses who kindly entrusted the stories of their traumas to me, and made them available for publication here; and indeed I dedicate it to all the other nurses who have been mentally wounded during the course of their caring for people in need.

Introduction

In June 1992 The International Society for Traumatic Studies held its first World Conference on psychotrauma in Amsterdam, under the title 'Trauma and Tragedy'. I attended the meeting in my capacity as a freelance psychologist attached to the Breda City Police department. Because I was also working for a community health care organization at the time, I looked through the congress folder in search of papers and workshops on the subject of psychotraumas amongst members of the nursing profession. Although there were more than 400 papers to be presented, my search was in vain. There were a number of papers on traumatic events experienced by firemen, police officers, train drivers, rescue teams, bank clerks, shop assistants, petrol pump attendants and soldiers, but nurses were not mentioned. I was surprised.

I had been working with nurses for ten years or more, and I had been struck by the fact that they were sometimes confronted by incidents which were no less stressful than those I had known among members of the police force. I also saw that nurses could be very shaken by them.

It was my sister-in-law, more than fifteen years earlier, who had first shown me just how deep these feelings can be. She had at the time been working for a year or more in a hospital, following the completion of her nursing training. One day she came to see me, obviously extremely distraught, and told me what had happened with an older patient she had been nursing. His physician had instructed her, as he had also previously instructed several of her colleagues, to give the patient a morphine injection to relieve his unbearable pain. The patient died an hour after she had given him the morphine injection. 'I have obviously killed him and it's my fault. What do I have to do now?'

Although I had all but completed my training as a psychologist, I knew as much about trauma support as the ordinary layman, and as far as I know no time had ever been allotted to the subject during the years of training. And, just as any layman would have done, I did my best to persuade my sister-in-law that she bore no responsibility whatsoever for the death of her patient, and that she therefore had no cause for concern. I did not succeed in putting her mind at rest, however, and nor did I in the talks that followed. Her guilt feelings remained rock-solid. She tried to resume her work but her fears that the incident would be repeated forced her to take sick leave. She did, in fact, consider giving up her work altogether, at the time. 'I am just no good for this sort of work', she would say again and again.

Six stressful months passed before she finally felt able to resume her work, and it was yet another six months before she was back to her old self again.

The more I recalled this and other incidents, during the course of the congress, the more amazed I became. And when this sense of amazement was joined by feelings of outrage, I decided the time had come to turn it into positive action and, therefore, set myself the task of writing a book about traumatic incidents as experienced by nurses in the course of their daily work. It had to be a book which, in addition to the necessary theoretical aspects, would also include a number of practical tips on how best to cope with traumatic events. The book also needed to provide space for nurses to tell their own stories, in their own ways. I felt this was important for several reasons. First, many who undergo these experiences tend to become isolated and feel ashamed of their own emotional reactions to them. Second, by reading accounts of what happened to others, they discover that the strange feelings they have are, in fact, very normal; they realize that they were not abnormal feelings arising from normal events, but rather normal feelings arising from abnormal events. Being aware of what others have experienced assists nurses first in learning from the mistakes of others and second in finding a suitable strategy for coming to terms with a shock event in his or her own life. The third therapeutic element of these personal accounts is the hope inherent in them. Traumatized nurses usually view the future with despair. Reading about someone else's experiences can show them that there really is a light at the end of the tunnel.

Obtaining these stories of personal experiences was not so easy. I had hoped to be able to gather stories quite easily and quickly via the nurses and assistant nurses I encountered in my daily work or whom I met at lectures and courses. During my quest for written accounts, it became repeatedly apparent just how difficult it is for nurses to break their silence and put their stories to paper. Some, it appeared, were afraid of difficulties with their employers; senior hospital and nursing home staff often equate open discussion of shock events as 'hanging your dirty washing on the line.' Most of the nurses I spoke to in my pursuit of personal stories felt unable to comply with my request because of the shame they felt about what had happened. This guilt/shame could not even be assuaged by my undertaking not to print names and to safeguard their anonymity by changing some of the basic data (e.g. place and date).

I realized that I was getting nowhere fast, and decided therefore to place an advertisement in *Verpleegkunde Nieuws* (Nursing News). In it, I announced my plan for this book and asked nurses and assistant nurses who had experienced some kind of shock event in the course of their work to contact me. The responses constitute the nine stories presented in Part 1 of this book. Five of them are based on written material which several nurses had sent to me. I have re-worked most of the stories to some extent, in order to make them more focused and more compact as case histories. The content, as such, has not been changed. I was thus an editor rather than an author.

Four nurses who responded to my advertisement informed me that they were unable to put their stories on paper, but were quite willing to talk about their experiences with me personally. I therefore made separate appointments with them, and wrote my own account of the information they had entrusted to me.

The section following the personal stories comprises a number of quotations from accounts of highly disturbing incidents which nursing staff have experienced in their work. They are drawn from the many telephone calls and letters I received after the publication of the Dutch version of this book.

Part 1 would not have been achieved without the selfless efforts of others, and Part 2 – albeit to a lesser degree – also relied on the work of others. The Reference list presents the books and articles which inspired and encouraged me in the writing of this book. Such a simple statement of the sources to which one refers hardly does justice to two publications in particular and which I found especially helpful. As a token of my gratitude, I will mention them separately here.

I based the section on the 'Recognition of psychotrauma' (Chapter 1) primarily on Lewis Herman's book *Trauma and Recovery*, and it is also worth mentioning here that this is one of the best books currently available on psychotrauma in general.

Table 1.5 and the three checklists given at the end of Chapter 2 are based partly on the brochure issued by Kent Social Services Department in England for the survivors, and their next of kin, of *The Herald of Free Enterprise* channel ferry disaster, which was in turn based on a leaflet produced for Bradford City Council.

My hope is that this book will be a source of help and encouragement to nurses and assistant nurses who have had the misfortune to have experienced very disturbing events in the course of their work. My wish too is that they will recover within a reasonable time and that they will be spared an unnecessarily long period of pain and suffering. I hope that this book will also provide useful tips for those wanting to help a colleague who has suffered such an event.

My work will also have been rewarded if this book succeeds, as I hope it will, in encouraging health institutions, still at the starting blocks, to develop a policy and procedures to ensure that individual staff members are given the necessary support and guidance they need in the aftermath of the type of situations addressed here.

Finally, a tip for anyone reaching for this book in a time of need: the most important information is contains can be found in the schedules given in Chapters 1 and 2, and in the three *check lists* in Chapter 2. These sections will provide anyone wanting fast access to relevant data with the initial information they need.

Part 1

Practice

Personal Accounts

1 The end of a nightmare

Agnes' story

All the nurses who responded to my request in *Verpleegkunde Nieuws* (Nursing News) and sent me their stories did so with an accompanying letter. For obvious reasons, these letters are not included here, but I have, with the writer's specific approval, made one exception. She writes:

> *'Dear Huub,*
>
> *Two weeks ago, I was having quite a battle with myself: I wanted to respond to your notice in **Verpleegkunde Nieuws** asking for nurses to send you accounts of traumatic moments they had encountered in the course of their work. And, in fact, when I read the announcement, I immediately thought: "Oh, I've got a very good one for you...", and I decided to telephone you. During our conversation, I was able to put it all into words quite well and I almost believed myself that I had come to terms very well with what had happened: everything was perfectly in order. Nothing, therefore, stood in the way of my putting it all down on paper, and I have never had great difficulty in expressing myself in writing. It all happened more than twenty years ago, after all.*
>
> *After brooding on it for a couple of weeks, however, I had to admit to myself that it was not going to work this time. I was not able to put pen to paper as I had thought, and I felt lacking: I had promised you. I telephoned you again and told you how impotent and thoroughly fed-up I felt. Having expressed my feelings in that way, my reluctance ebbed somewhat. Something important had happened during our talk: you said that I had suffered enough and you offered to help me formulate it more clearly. For the first time in years, I felt listened to. It meant, too, that I could really cry about it for the first time, and that of course did me a great deal of good. I am now, in consequence, able to commit my story to paper.*

Because I do not want to be confronted by all kinds of questions in my current working situation about this past experience, I have chosen to use a pseudonym.

What was it all about?

Some twenty years ago, I was working as a newly qualified Charge Nurse in the internal medicine department of an academic hospital. There was an intensive care ward attached to the department for patients needing special nursing care, including heart patients, sometimes on monitors. There were no central monitors at that time, only individual monitors at each bed, and in those days the nursing staff was expected, in principle, to remain on the ward all the time, so that patients could be constantly observed. It was, however, quite normal to leave the ward if there was no immediate need for intensive monitoring; and in this case, what you did was carefully to set the intensive care equipment at its lowest and highest limits, so that the alarm would go off at the slightest change in the patient's condition.

The kitchen-unit was opposite the ward and if you left both doors open, you still had a reasonable view of what was going on in the ward.

Things were very quiet that evening when I went on duty. There was one man who was shortly to be transferred to an ordinary ward and a new patient with a heart condition who was attached to the monitor and on a lidocaine drip. The situation appeared to be stable.

Things were still quiet later in the afternoon; everything was under control and I felt like having a cup of coffee. Having taken the necessary measures, I left the ward for the kitchen for a moment in order to make myself a cup of coffee and chat to one of my colleagues.

When I came back to the ward – I don't know how long I had been away: five or ten minutes perhaps? – I got the shock of my life. The new patient was in a very bad way – the drip was empty, his heartbeat was extremely irregular and his blood pressure was far too low. The monitor had not given the alarm because the frequency of the heartbeat, although irregular, was still within acceptable limits. I called for help and filled the drip again. Surely it had not been empty for very long? Surely I wasn't away for that long? The junior doctor on duty was there within a few minutes and asked me what had happened, and I told him.

A short time later, the patient had an attack of ventricular fibrillation, and he was defibrillated as fast as possible. All appeared to be going well. His heartbeat remained irregular, however, and the same crisis situation repeated itself a short time later. The patient rallied again, although his heart was still not beating normally. The situation was repeated something like eight times – or may be more – as the long evening progressed. There was no cardiologist on duty although the junior doctor did have telephone contact with him. In the end, my colleague and I were busy defibrillating the patient, whilst the junior doctor was on the telephone receiving instructions from the consultant.

The patient became very anxious, and after several defibrillation attempts he told me that he did not want any more: "Please, sister, don't do it any more". I will never forget the look on his face. And I? "We have to do it, Mr. Jones – it's for your own good." The defibrillation had burned his chest, and I took care not to let his wife, who had arrived at his bedside in the meantime, see the burns.

The situation became untenable for my colleague and I, and at a certain point, therefore, we asked the junior doctor to take the defibrillation over from us…but he had first to consult his superior. When he came back from the telephone (he must have felt pretty helpless), we informed him that we would not participate any more in the treatment. The patient died half an hour later. End of a nightmare?

The evening staff arrived on duty and we were able to tell the story of the evening's events, but because I was on early shift the following day, I did not stay too long. At home I talked to my husband, who was doing his internship in the same hospital at the time, about it and the sadness I felt. We agreed that it had been a very unfortunate situation and that these kinds of moments are part and parcel of our profession. Talk about feeling helpless!

It was very busy on the ward the next day. There was some talk of what had happened the day before, and quite honestly I didn't feel any strong need to relate the events in detail again. I remember thinking: "there will be time for that later".

At the end of the day duty, I went home dead tired. Outside the hospital building, I saw the deceased patient's wife walking a few metres ahead of me, and she was extremely tearful. She hailed a taxi and, sobbing loudly, informed the taxi-driver that her life had no further meaning for her, because she had lost what was most dear to her. At that moment, all I wanted was for the ground to open and swallow me up – because it was all my fault. Something broke in me; I froze to the ground. I have not talked about it since, not for years, and no one has ever asked me about it again.

The period that followed

I suffered nightmares for months; it was something threatening, but I could never get a real "picture" of it. I always woke up bathed in sweat and heart pounding. I talked to no one about it – it was my own fault, after all.

In retrospect, however, I realize that from that point onward I was no longer able to respond adequately to crisis situations. A wall came down – I couldn't think clearly, or I would start to shake. Such behaviour is of course totally unacceptable on an intensive care ward and I am not sure whether the people around me had any inkling of it. No one has ever made any comments to me about it.

When my husband joined a GP practice in another part of the country, I of course followed him; I left my job and concentrated my energies on my family and on his practice. I told anyone who wanted to hear it that I missed my nursing work, but it wasn't true – I was pleased to be rid of it.

Since then, and right up to the present day, I have avoided crisis situations surrounding illness and accidents and so forth. One such moment – again several years ago – is still imprinted in my mind. My neighbour suffered a cardiac arrest whilst working in his garden – his GP did not arrive in time to resussitate him and he died. I was taking a walk with my children when it happened, and when I came home and heard what had happened, panic struck. To those around I said how sorry I was not to have been at home at the time because I might have been able to save him. But deep in my heart, I was glad not to have been there…and that thought, of course, left me feeling guilty again.

I was able, during this period, to talk to a doctor sometimes about what had happened in the hospital. He did his best to reassure (?!) me by saying that the man could not have been saved anyway and that there was no reason to feel uneasy about it. And that gave me yet more reason to push the event as far into the background as possible. I didn't want to have to think about it any more and I felt that I really should put it behind me now. *Up to the present time, therefore, people have only heard the rational side of my story.*

Here and now

Now that it is all coming back into my mind again, I am shocked by my own reactions. I have been sleeping badly and restlessly during the last few weeks, and I keep walking around wondering what is really bothering me so much. I sit in front of my PC, with clammy hands and palpitations. In actual fact, I don't want to think about it at all. What is wrong with me?

I suspect that initially I suppressed the whole event in my mind, and approached and coped with it later as a purely mental exercise. And now, after all those years, I am confronted by the emotions. It is not so strange that it happened following a difficult period in my life; it seems that I am more sensitive for old traumas and the emotions that accompany them. I still feel guilty about what happened and I am still angry about the way in which medical help was given in that situation. I still work in the social sector, where of course this sort of thing also happens.

I want to approach the matter with a positive attitude: I realize that this is one of the moments in my life which has taught me how important it is to express one's emotions. I am always aware of the fact that it is not good to have let this event lie dormant for so long and I wouldn't want the same thing to happen to others. In the meantime, I am again employed in the social sector, this time in education. My teaching includes both theory and practice and I have often tried to convince my students that they should talk about what troubles them, and that they are not the only ones with a problem! I also realize that I have discussed with my students many scary situations which have arisen in the course of my work (in order to stimulate fruitful group discussions), but that I have never mentioned this one event.

It has obviously had even more influence on my life than I realized. And now when I think about it, I recognize behaviour patterns in myself which make me wonder why I often made such a fuss about things. For example: I am a perfectionist by nature and I do not permit myself to make any mistakes in my work. The event I am talking about has obviously not encouraged me to take things more easily, and perhaps bringing it back to mind will help me now...'

2 Someone grabbed me from behind

Marijke's story

The following incident took place in a large psychogeriatric nursing home in the south of Holland. Marijke, a senior night charge nurse, is heading a team of five on the evening in question. Each night charge nurse is responsible for one ward, and Marijke and an assistant night charge nurse circulate through the building, ready to assist where necessary. The story opens on 2 November 1988.

A leakage in the cellar

'It is my last evening on night duty, and I will then be off duty for three weeks. It is a good evening with a good atmosphere amongst all my colleagues. A few days ago, a leakage had been reported in the cellar of the nursing home, and a bucket has been placed under the drip in order to avoid flooding and water damage. I have been asked to check once or twice a night and to empty the bucket when necessary. The cellar has a side-door which residents can use to enter the nursing home after 11 o'clock in the evening. If residents return late, the taxi brings them to the cellar door and rings the bell, and one of the staff on duty will then go down and open the door.

At half past two I suddenly remember that I had not yet been to the cellar, and before going down I go to the first ward to tell the night charge nurse there that I will be downstairs for a moment. "When I come back, we'll have a cup of coffee together", I say. And as I happily trot down to the cellar and I go inside, I am suddenly aware that someone is standing behind me, and before I can look round, two hands grab me. My first reaction is that one of my colleagues is playing a joke on me. I look over my shoulder and see a fairly tall, blond man. It gives me an awful shock, and in my fear I give out a terrible scream. The man loosens his grip on me, I tear myself free and make a run for it. I take the stairway and run to the first floor. "Someone grabbed me, there was someone in the cellar" is all I can stammer in front of the charge nurse with whom I was going to have a cup of coffee. It was only then that I realized that I had a radiophone with me and decided to call my male colleague higher in the building. When he rings back I can hardly get any words out of my mouth; the charge nurse takes the radiophone from me and asks him to come immediately. His first reaction too is that it is some kind of a joke, but as soon as he understands the situation, he is downstairs in a wink.

The first thing he does is telephone the police, and after that the head of the nursing service, a nun resident in a nearby convent and always on call. He tells her what has happened and asks her to come, and he remains with me until the police arrive. With my heart in my mouth, we then go to the cellar – only for a moment, though, because I can't take it for long, and I say "May I go please, I never want to come here again". I am allowed to go. While the police go in search of the burglar, or any trace of him, I make my way to a department on the other side of the building. I want to be as far away from the cellar as I can. I wait there with one of my colleagues for the arrival of the head of the nursing service, drinking a lot of coffee in the meantime. She arrives, in a state of panic, within half an hour: "It is good that this is your last evening on duty. Now you will have three weeks in which to catch your breath." My response is "I don't think I will ever do any night duty again," and my colleague replies in the same way as the colleagues I speak to later: "As long as the colleague who takes over from you tomorrow doesn't hear about it." And as long as this person, or that person, doesn't hear about it. We are all so afraid that all we want to do is lock the door and disappear. Our fear has lessened somewhat when the police – together with the nursing home director, who has been called from his bed – return in order to draw up the official report. I am relieved that they are prepared to allow plenty of time for this. Before they leave, they give me a small brochure issued by the Victim-help Bureau, and at 6 o'clock I go home, an hour earlier than usual.

My husband, whom I had rung whilst waiting for the police, had got up early and prepared a cup of coffee for me. When he leaves for his work an hour later than usual, I go to bed, but cannot sleep. The images of what had happened to me, kept coming back into my mind and made it impossible for me to sleep. My husband comes home at 1 o'clock; he has taken the afternoon off so that we can go to the nursing home together. I had told him in the morning that the police would be at the nursing home and that they would probably have more questions for me. Wild elephants, however, would not get me to the nursing home now, and I tell my husband that "If they need me, they can come here".

I feel a different person in the days that follow; I am short-tempered and easily irritated. One wrong word, an ashtray or vase ten centimetres out of line, and I can explode. I am unreasonable. All I want is for everyone to leave me alone. I can't help it, but my thoughts drift back continually to the incident. In the weeks before, my head had been filled with the fact that it was no longer possible to cope with our only son and that he would have to be placed in a special home, and the whole matter troubled me deeply. The incident in the nursing home has come at a very difficult moment for me. The people around me can't see how unhappy I am. If I go outside, they seem to say: "She waves to everyone, she does the garden, she dresses nicely, she must be okay". I am wearing a mask, and I say to myself "That's enough, it's over now". I could never bear to hear people whining (because talking about one's difficulties was whining, as far as I was concerned).

I have three weeks before the next period of night duty. During the day I often go to the shopping centre in the town. I keep looking round and I notice that I am constantly looking for a blond, solidly-built, man. But why? Not to be able to deliver him to the police or to give him a good whip of my tongue – assuming that I could, or would have the courage to do it – but to ask him "Why did you do it? Did you want to play a joke on me by giving me a shock like that, or did you want to rob me? Or assault me perhaps?" There are other questions too which still occupy my mind: "Why me? Why not someone with more money or more jewellery? Why not someone more attractive or younger?"

The nursing home fills me with dread. If I have to go somewhere, I keep as far away from it as possible, and I don't even mind making a wide detour to avoid it. Some days after the incident, the nursing home telephones me and asks me to call in. I say I can't, and stay at home. The following day I am visited at home by the head of the nursing service and she presents me with a letter from the directors. It is addressed to all employees, and the first two sentences are: "As you will have been informed already, a disturbing incident occurred in the nursing home on the night of 2 November. The police inspected the whole building and have come to the conclusion that the outside doors were locked." What really happened is not explained.

My mind is made up: I want another job. I suddenly have no interest in my present work. I will never feel safe on night duty again. My function as head night charge nurse, is extra difficult for me: I always have to set an example to others. As head, the final responsibility for everything lies with me. I would prefer to work under the head. That offers some protection. I set about writing letters of application. The prospect of my first period of night duty after the incident hangs like a dark cloud over me. I dare not take it on yet. I am still entitled to some holiday and decide to take it now.

Back to work

Another three weeks pass, and I reach the moment of truth – there is no getting away from it. Fortunately my male colleague on the evening in question is also on duty, and thanks to that I am able to get myself over the threshold. I do not discuss the incident at work. I don't want to cause any anxiety among my colleagues. I put on a brave face. When a colleague does ask me about what happened, however, I fence her off by saying that everything is all right and that it can happen anywhere. My colleagues do not pursue the matter, and deep in my heart it disappoints me. My feeling is that they really do want to talk about it, and they do want to know what happened, but no one dares. The only one who really shows me any support is a religious Brother who is also a nurse; I don't have to say anything to him, he knows what I am feeling just by looking at me. When it all gets too much, he simply says "Would you like to have a meal here tonight? Don't be afraid". But I don't talk about the incident, even with him.

If I have to let one of the residents in at the cellar entrance, I ensure that I am never alone; I always ring for one of my colleagues first. If I have to go and see a colleague on another ward, I begin to cough or hum ten metres away, because I don't want to make her jump by appearing suddenly. This is probably just a reflection of my own shock reaction, but I can't help it and I will never lose this habit, however long I work in this nursing home.

The directors have informed the personnel, but not the residents. The motive is: "We don't want to disturb their peace." In the meantime, I am aware that among the personnel, the wildest rumours about that evening of 2 November are flying around. I want the directors to take swift action in introducing a number of security measures so that the chances of a repeat incident are kept to a minimum. Nothing happens, however. I therefore decide to write a letter to the Staff Council, suggesting a number of steps that could be taken, such as a lamp which signals when the cellar door is unlocked at night, and which automatically goes on when someone approaches the door from outside. I send a copy of the letter to the office of the staff/resident *Newsletter* and I also write an article describing what happened on the night of 2 November.

I am very annoyed by the fact that no one, it appears, wants or is allowed to talk about it, and because of this all kinds of nonsense is being circulated, such as "Marijke has been robbed", or "Marijke has been raped". I want my article to put a stop to all these rumours.

A few days later, I receive a letter from the directors in which they write that "after detailed consultation" they had decided not to allow publication of my letter or my article in the *Newsletter*. Their decision is explained as follows: "Although we can well imagine that you feel a need to clarify the situation and to refute the stories, we expect that the opposite will be achieved by publishing your letter and article. We are of the opinion that it would not be advisable now to re-direct attention to an incident which happened four months ago and which is fading from the minds of many." The directors obviously want to do a major cover-up.

I feel misunderstood and isolated. I can't tell my story to the personnel (and I admit that my putting on a brave face is to blame for this) and the possibility of discussing the incident with the residents has also now been blocked for all time. I would very probably find understanding and a willing ear in that quarter. And I cannot load my story onto my family or friends any more. They will think I am whining. "Are you still talking about that (again)?!" I don't want to complain and I therefore keep my mouth shut. I have tried for a long time to get my husband to talk about it with me, but he always comes with the (well-intended) comment: "Marijke, why don't you just go into town", or "Do this or do that". Apart from my husband, I have also spoken to my mother about what happened, but that was right at the beginning, and in front of her I also restrain myself now.

The old atmosphere at work has gone. We used to work well together and we had a lot of fun, but that has gone too. There are no more jokes, no more teasing.

Fourteen months after the incident, I finally manage to find another job. During my last evening on night duty, New Year's Eve 1990, I am given a police questionnaire, asking for suggestions for night-time security. It throws me completely off-balance: only after fourteen months is something being done. My husband writes a letter to the nursing home directors saying what a wonderful goodbye-present it is, a questionnaire like that. He receives a reply a few days later. The directors inform us that the police have been very busy, and that is why it has taken so long, and that they regret that the questionnaire arrived at such an unfortunate moment for me.

A new start, or history repeats itself

I have a new job, but that does not mean that I have left my past completely behind me. Even now, four years after the event, I am sometimes reminded of it. If I am standing in a queue at the supermarket and someone knocks against me with a trolley, I am furious. I want space around me, especially behind me. And if I am approached from behind, I blow my top – such as happened a year ago. We were having a drink after work and one of the men (a very nice person indeed) wanted to surprise me by coming up behind and putting his hands over my eyes and saying "Hi Marijke, who am I?". I explode completely and throw all kinds of verbal abuse at him. My colleagues look at me as if to say: "What's the matter with her all of a sudden?" When I have calmed down, I feel deeply ashamed – he did not deserve that at all. I draw him away from the group and say: "Listen, I'm terribly sorry, but something happened to me some time ago which really frightened me. It is not your fault that I responded as I did. Please forgive me."

During the same period that this happened, about a year ago, I was confronted by yet another incident.

I am following an evening course. One evening in May, I decided that because it was such lovely weather, I would walk there instead of going by car. It is only a fifteen minute walk. I put my lesson papers in my handbag with my keys, diary and purse, and halfway to the school, someone snatches the bag from my arm. A fraction of a second later, I see a youth on a motorbike dashing off with my handbag.

History repeats itself. In the days that followed, I was terribly anxious and panicky. I keep asking myself: Why? And why me?'

3 The period that followed was awful

Janine's story

'I work as a nursing assistant in a residential care centre. Two years ago I was called by one of the helpers because "one of the residents had become unwell in the shower". It was well known that this lady suffered from periods of manic depression, and when I got to her it became apparent that she had hanged herself.

The period that followed was awful. When I got home in the evenings, the first thing I did was to turn the light on in the hall, and from the hall I would reach for the light in the shower by sliding my hand around the doorway and pulling on the light cord. And after that, I did the same in the living room and the bedroom. This was followed by checking to see if there was anything untoward in the shower. If I woke up during the night, there was no way I would leave my bed, no matter how great the need.

I often relived the event in my sleep, and if I woke I would read for a while as a distraction. In the morning I would make my way very carefully to the shower, having first of all turned on every light in the house. My family asked if I would prefer to sleep at their homes, but I didn't want to do that because I knew that at some time or other I would have to return to my own home.

I became very jittery, especially when I had to distribute the medicines on the floor concerned. At every sound, I would take a quick look behind me, thinking to myself: 'If only this floor was finished'.

Later whenever I had to help another resident take a shower in the same room, I would often try to change to another shower or with another colleague (the double accommodation areas consisted of two single rooms each with its own shower). And if the door of the shower in question was open, I would close it. Wild elephants wouldn't have got me into that room again. If you have a late shift, you have to work from 17.00–17.30 hours "alone" in the home and I always preferred to avoid this shift, because I found it very frightening.

When a resident appears to be missing, I will never be the first to check the shower. As a means of self-protection, I always let a colleague go in first, even now. And if there is a TV programme on suicide, I make a video of it and watch it during the day, so that it is less frightening. There are some television programmes which I never watch any more and I also find it difficult to talk about this experience during the hours of darkness.

I would have liked to have read the letter our suicide resident left behind, not simply out of curiosity but rather to understand the "why" of it.

It seems that the matter has been forgotten at my work, because no one refers to it any more. Although it does fade slowly, my anxiety will always remain.'

4 I fight back with all the strength I have

Baukje's story

Baukje worked as a psychiatric nurse in a Psychiatric Hospital, on a closed clinical ward for young people. She was once confronted in her work by such a threatening situation that she was on sick leave for several months. It happened three years ago.

Evening duty

'I have night duty on the day in question and I have just completed my training. During the change of nursing shifts, I am informed that a colleague is ill and that someone else will be called in for that evening, a young man who had just completed his Registered General Nursing training and this was to be his first experience on a psychiatric ward. Another colleague would start at six o'clock in the evening; it is, as always, very busy on the ward and now I had to do practically all the work alone until he arrived.

A male patient, who has been psychotic for several days, is very difficult this shift. He follows me around constantly and accuses me of stealing his mind, and says that in the eyes of God I am an evil person. He becomes steadily more threatening. I try to keep a reasonable conversation going, and initially it has some effect.

In the evening, when my colleague has arrived, the situation gets completely out of hand. The patient informs me that he intends to murder me and the world will thus be saved. I am busy in the office when I see him coming. He starts by banging the window of my office with a radio flex and demands that I come out so that he can kill me.

I lock the door and telephone colleagues on other wards to warn them that I need urgent help. I try to boost my courage by reminding myself that the patient cannot reach me so long as the door is locked. I can see through the window (looking out over the ward – see drawing) that the other patients on the ward are beginning to cheer and clap. They shout that I'm "chicken" and a coward because I dare not leave the office. Loudly encouraged, the patient continues to bang on the window, whilst I hope and pray that my colleagues will soon arrive. I'm imprisoned and suddenly, to my great relief, I notice that the patient has stopped banging on the window and is walking back to the ward.

For fear that he may now attack one of the other patients, I decide to leave my office…and I regret it immediately. The moment I step outside my office, the patient turns again in my direction and lunges towards me. He tries to push me to the ground and get the radio flex around my neck. I do my best to put up a resistance and defend myself, and I fight back with all the strength I have. I find myself able to call on reserves of strength I didn't know I had.

Actually, I succeed quite well in defending myself, despite the fact that the patient is considerably taller and certainly much stronger than I am. In a flash, in the middle of the struggle, I see that two other patients are coming to help him and the newly qualified Assistant Nurse, jumps in to help me against the three attackers. Once other colleagues have arrived to help, things move very fast and everything is soon under control again.

(I heard later that one of my colleagues who was working in the kitchen, had seen it all happen but was too frightened to leave the kitchen. This means that she did nothing to help me – and this was a great shock and disappointment to me later.)

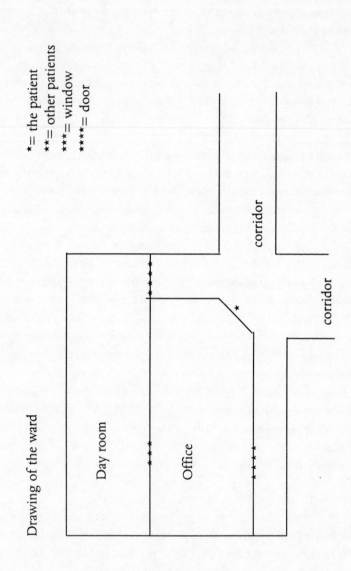

Drawing of the ward

Day room

Office

corridor

corridor

*= the patient
**= other patients
***= window
****= door

The consequences

When I arrive home after my shift, I find a colleague and good friend waiting for me. One of my other colleagues on the ward had telephoned him and asked him to give me initial help and support, and we talk the whole night about what happened. At 6 am I decide to take sick leave. I simply cannot face going back to the ward – after all, everyone is against me there.

And it was after having made this decision that the real misery began. I can hardly sleep any more at night, and if I do manage to fall asleep the nightmares soon wake me up again and bathe me in sweat. I often find myself walking the streets at night in total despair. I feel terrible and the daylight hours bring no respite. I do nothing at all the whole day, and everything passes me by. I have stopped living, in fact. Colleagues and friends do their best to cheer me up, but wherever they take me, or whatever we do, I have no pleasure in it – I feel depressed and anxious. I have the feeling that I have failed. And at night especially I often relive that image of the cheering and clapping patients goading the attacker on. I feel utterly helpless.

I sleep better after a month or more, but it is certainly another three months before I can face life again. And only after three and a half months am I able to resume my work.

I receive a great deal of support from my friends and colleagues during this period. Particularly by talking in great detail about what had happened am I able slowly but surely to distance myself from it. It is certainly a full year before I am able to give it its rightful place in my life, and before it no longer controls my whole existence.

And now

I still work on the same ward, and with pleasure, I am glad to say. There is of course a lot more that can be said about it. So much happens with one's "self" following an experience like this, that one could actually write a whole book about it.'

5 You can just sit and read the paper

Yvonne's (community nurse) story

'I and a colleague are responsible for the nursing care of a man who is handicapped as a result of childhood polio; he can no longer walk and has become more and more bent with age. Because his lungs were being put under such pressure, it was decided that he should undergo a major back operation, followed by nine months in bed in plaster. He can do nothing for himself and, in addition to community nursing, he also has a home-help. My colleague and I share the nursing task, because it is quite demanding. The man is not only in a bad way physically, but also socially and emotionally. He is, in fact, in a midlife-crisis in which he can only look ahead to pain, loneliness and invalidity.

We are struck by the fact that despite his frail body and his invalidity, he still manages to be somewhat macho in his behaviour. He has strict ideas, for instance, about man/woman roles. He also talks a lot about his problems, but refuses to accept more specific help from a social worker, for instance. My colleague and I have agreed amongst ourselves to adopt a listening stance and to avoid giving the impression that we can offer solutions.

As I get to know him better, he starts to talk about sexuality. He tells me that he was once a member of a "handicapped people and sexuality" work group. He confides to me too that until recently he had had a LAT (living apart together) relationship which lasted for several years. He is concerned that he can no longer give expression to his love or sexual needs. What can I do? I listen, show sympathy and share his hope that the back operation will have been successful and that he will become just as mobile as he was before.

My colleague is moving house and leaves the team. The patient returns to the hospital so that the pins can be removed and work can start on rehabilitating him. Before he is admitted he thanks me for the care and attention I have given him, and stresses that he regarded me as a trusted friend with whom he could talk about anything and everything. He asks if he may telephone me at home.

I don't want that, however, and refer him instead to the telephone-surgery service.

Uninterrupted talking

Shortly after the pin-removal operation, he suffers a heart attack, and it is four months before he is home again. The rehabilitation process is more difficult than he expected. The home care programme now comprises three disciplines: a home-help, a physiotherapist and myself as community nurse.

At first, I visit him on a daily basis for the necessary physical nursing care. My plan is to cut down the degree of care, and step by step I teach him to wash himself and take a shower, as he did before. He is often irritable and makes all kinds of demands on when I can and cannot come. He is extremely depressed, but he cannot reconcile asking people to help him with his problems, with his own sense of masculinity.

There comes a moment when we find ourselves in conflict. He accuses me of neglecting him, by which he means that he misses me as a discussion-partner now that I don't come so often, and that when I do come it is only in the interests of his physical nursing needs. We come to an agreement that I will call in for a talk in the afternoon. And from now on, it all goes wrong.

He telephones me more often to ask if I will visit him in the afternoon for a talk. "Then we can talk without being interrupted", meaning that the home-help and the physiotherapist will not be there. My colleagues also begin to notice the frequency of his telephone calls. "Your boy friend has 'phoned again", they say jokingly. And I hate it. I cut the number of my visits, by lengthening the periods in between, and finally I put a complete stop to them just before the onset of the main summer holiday period. He is still very depressed, and although I have frequently drawn his attention to better help possibilities for this, he has always refused to make use of them.

Six months after he was removed from our care-list, he phoned me one day, in panic and crying, to ask me if I could visit him. I am not sure what to do; I don't feel like going to see him at all, but on the other hand I feel unable to refuse. There are quite a few new people in our team and I don't want to burden them with this complicated situation. I decide therefore that I will have to visit him, and once again he starts on about his sexual feelings. In the past, he used to masturbate under the shower, but he dare not do this any more because he is afraid of having another heart attack. He asks me if I will stay close to the shower as he masturbates under the shower. "You can just sit and read the newspaper...". It is just a question of reassuring himself that he will be okay. I want to have the matter over as fast as possible and say to him: "okay, I'll read the paper while you get on with it". My heart is thundering and I leave the room. A few minutes later I hear a scream from the bathroom. Something has gone wrong. I run to the bathroom, he can't reach a climax and will I help him. Now, finally, I am really angry and I leave the house.

Muddling on for too long

In the time after this moment, I keep hearing this sentence in my head: "I don't want to have anything to do with that man ever again". I am nervous and afraid that he will call for our help again, and I know that in that case, I will be the one who will have to go to him. I know too that I will then have to bring up the subject of this incident. I dare not discuss it with my colleagues – they know nothing.

The fact that I am facing this situation alone is the most difficult part for me. And there are several reasons why I dare not talk about it. A year ago, I suggested to the team that we should discuss the subject of sexuality together. I suggested it because of a spastic patient who occasionally had an erection while being nursed, although he could do nothing about it himself. My suggestion was greeted with derision by my colleagues. The atmosphere among the team is also not very good. There have been rumblings of discontent for some time. There is no one with whom I feel entirely at ease. We have had no head of department for some time, and that means that I cannot look for help in that direction either.

I do, however, discuss the matter with three people outside the team: my boy friend, and two friends who are both hospital nurses. My boy friend is very decisive in his reaction: "If I could get my hands on that man…"; his intention of course is to show support, but the statement as such is of no use to me at all. My two girl friends are shocked by my story, but they also have no real answer to the problem.

The problem, of course, more or less solves itself in due course. Six months later I leave the team, and the man did not telephone us during that time. There was no need, therefore, to discuss the matter with my colleagues.

If I look back at this situation, I blame myself for allowing it to go on for so long. I should have defended my boundaries better and not allow myself to believe that I could achieve more with this patient than I could with others.'

6 No patient would do such a thing

Kirsten's story

'Perhaps I really will have to make a start on something I have never written about before. St. Elizabeth's Hospital! It happened several times, in the time that I worked there as a student nurse and with different patients too. All male.

I don't know how it will appear on paper. Probably in a way that only I can understand. But that doesn't really matter; I am the only one who *needs* to understand it!

As a student nurse, I was always very sociable and a good colleague. Some people even felt that I exaggerated somewhat. Looking back, they may have been jealous that I was so well-liked by most of the patients. Whatever the case may be, I always did anything for anyone and sometimes even worked complete extra shifts. I was there for the patients one hundred per cent, and I put a lot of time into the "talking aspect". Patients always have many problems which seem to surface in times of sickness or approaching death. I always had a great deal of time for the dying patients. In these cases, I could quite easily sit for hours on the edge of their beds, listening to them. Some patients, men especially, wanted the curtains drawn round the bed, because they didn't want others to see them crying. And if that was their wish, I simply drew the curtains as they asked. It never occurred to me that something like this could ever create problems.

The patient responsible for the problem in the end was a man in his fifties. He was very unhappy, and this was why I was prepared to listen to him. When the tears started to fall, I saw that he was feeling ill at ease. I suggested, therefore, that I draw the curtains, and he was pleased about that. He sat, half lying, in bed and I sat diagonally to him on the edge of the bed. After three-quarters of a hour, he had regained his composure and I was planning to bring the conversation to a close. I had other things to do and there were other patients needing attention. Just as I was about to stand up, he laid his arm on my leg and asked me if I would stay a little longer. I replied, however, that I really had to move on. When he said that he just wanted to say one more thing, I decided to remain seated for a while. He began to chatter about nothing at all. And all of a sudden it started. He sat straight up in bed and put his hand under the skirt of my uniform. I was shocked and wanted to stand up. He immediately grabbed my arm and said "ssst". I was terribly frightened. He was very strong. I noticed that my arm was blue where he had grasped it. I felt his fingers inside me. I began to cry and then he stopped. "Sorry, you mustn't cry, I thought this was what you wanted", he said. "Don't tell anyone, or else I will deny everything and turn the whole thing around."

The whole incident lasted no more than 30 seconds. A few months later I was raped by a man I did not know, not in the hospital but on my way home. It happened when I returned home after a party, and by mistake I got off the bus one stop too soon, quite close to my parents' house. I suffered hell at the time because my menstruation stopped for two months following the rape, and I dared not tell anyone about it. Fortunately, my periods did return later. Because I only want to write at this point about what happened in St. Elizabeth's Hospital, I will not say anything further about this here. More things happened in this hospital after the rape.

'This is for you'

The incident I want to talk about first took place about six months later. This time it happened in the bathroom. I was helping a man get undressed for the shower. He sat on the shower stool with his pyjamas around his ankles and I sat on my haunches pulling his trousers over his feet, when he suddenly had an erection. It gave me quite a fright, but I carried on as if nothing had happened. When he said: "This is for you", I felt quite frightened. I tried to keep calm and pretended I hadn't heard him. He responded by pressing my face against his penis and saying: "Go on, that's what it's for". I tore myself loose and fell backwards onto the floor. I then pulled the alarm bell because I wanted to get away, but it was my own bleeper which went off, so that didn't help me. For medical reasons, I could not leave the patient alone, and I therefore opened the door and asked the first nurse who passed by, if she would keep her eye on things for a moment. I left and did not return. I was later reprimanded by the head of the department. The fact that I did not return to the patient was written into my training-book as seriously irresponsible behaviour. I did not tell anyone what had really happened.

Another incident, also after the rape, occurred when I was making up the bed of a bed-ridden patient. The curtains were drawn and I was changing the under-sheet. Patients have to turn onto their sides for this. If you are alone, you have to be on the patient's (face) side of the bed, and if possible work across him. Whilst I bent over him, in one rapid movement he had undone the press-studs on my uniform and pulled my bra up. It all happened within a fraction of a second. When I was upright again, my breasts were bare and he was touching them with his "dirty" hands. I pulled my uniform closed as best I could and ran out of the ward. I hastily called to a colleague telling her where I was going, and ran on without waiting for her reply. Straight to the bathroom. I stood under the shower for hours and hoped I would disappear through the drain.

I had a few days off after that. And I needed them. Again I did not talk to any of my colleagues or the head of my department,

and again I was severely reprimanded for leaving a patient unat-
tended.

Even after that I still did not tell anyone. I had no witnesses,
after all. Who would believe me, any way? No patient would do
such a thing.

A 37-year-old American

It is now roughly two years ago since this all happened, but what
happened to me then still invades my mind several times a day. If
there is a TV programme about a hospital or medical matters, or I
see sex scenes in a film, everything I experienced in St. Elizabeth's
comes back again. I immediately turn the television off or switch
over to another channel.

I am also terribly "edgy". A window or door suddenly closing,
an unexpected sound, a bell ringing, all these things scare me.
Actually I am tensed-up the whole day long.

I am never aggressive, at least not physically. I would never hit
anyone, but lately I can can really lash out with my tongue.
Especially towards people whom I know would never dream of
"dumping" me. Such as my parents and my sister. I am often really
"bitchy" towards them. I also feel I have become very cynical. And
very suspicious. I seldom look directly at people, but I keep a close
watch on them from the corner of my eyes. I am very much on my
guard, against men especially. To tell the truth, I wouldn't trust any
man again. Deep in my heart, I feel terrible anger towards men.
Sometimes when I am behind the wheel of my car and I see a man
on a zebra crossing, I get the sudden feeling of: "Now I can get
you". Fortunately, I have always been able to control myself up to
now.

I have slept badly for years. I often have very frightening
dreams. I also do not eat normally. Sometimes I can go for a whole
week without eating. It doesn't bother me at all. And then
suddenly, I start gorging myself until the fridge is completely
empty.

Perhaps I wouldn't be where I am now if I had talked to my
colleagues at the time about what happened to me. I have already

mentioned the fact that I did not talk about it because I was afraid they would not believe me. But there is another reason why I kept my mouth shut. And this has to do with an incident I had experienced at the start of my training. At that time I received a card, quite "out of the blue" from a former patient, a 37-year-old American who had had a heart attack and I had nursed him with great devotion. He had written on the card in English: "I owe you an orgasm". I was very upset by this and showed the card to my colleagues. Their reaction, however, was very cool and almost accusatory: "Something like that could only happen to you". And it taught me a lesson. If one's colleagues react like that, how could I expect their support in subsequent and similar incidents?

Despite all these events, I still think nursing is a wonderful profession. Truly.

What happened to me in my nursing work (and outside it) has probably, somehow or other, all been my own fault. I must have unconsciously provoked it in some way. Men are also partly to blame. That's the way they are. Not to be trusted.

What I find particularly upsetting is that I have lost all my trust in people. I would not wish on anyone what I have gone through in the last few years.'

7 'You shouldn't think about it any more'

Paul's story

'For the last four years, I have been working as a team leader in a closed ward of a hospital for chronic psychiatric patients. In addition to the unit for 12 patients, there are also two crisis rooms for emergency admission.

My story begins two years ago when one of our female patients, in her mid-thirties, committed suicide; it is discovered by one of my colleagues. He can see through the glass-pane in the door of the isolation cell that something is wrong, but before going inside he immediately goes for help. Quite by chance I am the first person he meets in the corridor, and I go at once to have a look. The first thing I do is telephone the GP. That same afternoon, when I return from visiting the family, I say: 'We should make a kind of scenario book containing instructions on how everyone involved in such an incident should be informed and helped. This would concern, first of all, the family, the co-patients and the colleagues. The book should state what should be done from the moment the suicide is discovered up to – for instance – two weeks later.'

When something serious occurs, all sorts of organizational, legal and technical matters have to be dealt with. And, in addition, there is need for emotional support and help. In our hospital, nothing at all has been done at this level, and it means that it is very unclear who, within the institution, should be informed. My suggestion that this kind of scenario book should be compiled is rejected out of hand, 'You shouldn't try to regulate things like that. You should simply leave people alone after a shock event. Everyone copes with it in his or her own way. One person will go and sit quietly in the corner, another will be busy doing all sorts of things, and another will want to talk, etc.' And that is as far as it gets.

Looking back – now two years on – I realize that it made a deep impact on me. I was the only one of the team to have seen the dead body. I had invested a great deal of energy in this woman, I had been through many moments with her, absurd things too, and sometimes in her psychotic periods I had received blows from her…and now suddenly she was not there any more. All kinds of emotions rose to the surface in me, such as pity and aggression, but I did not get the chance to work them through. Not intensely or long enough, in any case. And that was not good.

A little more than a year later, a 35-year-old man, who had already been with us for nine months, committed suicide by hanging himself on the handgrip above his bed. He had also made a serious suicide attempt nine months before he came to us, when he had jumped from a viaduct, resulting in two broken legs and serious concussion. We had a hard time with him, and he almost literally got under our skin. And then suddenly he ends it all.

The body is once again discovered by one of my colleagues. He asks me to join him and together we cut the rope with which the patient had hanged himself on the handgrip. In rounding-off all the necessary formalities of this suicide case, I am reminded constantly of the previous case. And again I propose to the department head that we should be much more aware of the consequences of this kind of experience, and that the team leaders should be given the chance to work it through, come to terms with it, and help each other. But once again, there is no response. The department head adds an extra argument this time, namely that my own team members are against it. This is, however, too dogmatic a statement. My impression is that some of my team are not enthusiastic because they want to cope with the event in their own way and that others are simply afraid to face their own emotions and work them through. Whatever the case may be, my suggestion is again pushed aside.

The second suicide is followed by a third, five weeks later. This time it is a woman aged about 40, whom we find lying face down on the bed with a strip of sheeting round her head. After this suicide, I tell my superior that the time has now definitely come for the team, as a whole, to meet and talk together about what has happened within a comparatively short space of time. And this time, our message was heard. The whole team is invited to spend two days on the coast, plus the psychiatrist, the treating psycho-therapist and our supervisor. These brain-storming days take place three months after the last suicide. I am unfortunately not able to be present because the days fall right in the middle of my autumn holiday.

I learn later from my colleagues that the suicides were not discussed at all during those days at the seaside. Another burning issue was the main subject of discussion. Eight months earlier, a young man was admitted to our unit with the label never-to-be-treated-in-the-group. He had the reputation of being extremely dangerous.

He is transferred to us from another department in the hospital where, in the time that he was there, he had attacked a considerable number of patients and colleagues. (He had attacked one patient so badly that the patient's cheekbone was shattered.) The young man is placed in the corner of the department where he is treated in isolation: in a separate closed unit (within our closed depart-ment), with its own isolation cell.

The discussion during those days on the coast centred on whether or not the young man should remain in our department, in terms of: is he not too great a responsibility for us? I am dwelling on this point because the same situation applies as in the suicide cases: *do you or do you not take the nursing staff seriously?*

I will explain this further. From the moment the young man was placed in our care, I told my colleagues: "Talk about your feelings. Don't behave as if you are not afraid when you have to enter his room. Don't go in if your courage fails you, ask a colleague to go with you. Tell each other how you feel when you have been with the patient, say if you were tense or not." In short, I tried in this situation too to stimulate my colleagues to express their emotions.

And in this, I stand in direct opposition to the management team, who feel that the personnel should do everything possible to put up a strong front in cases like these. The attitude of the psychiatrist, who was also with the group on the coast, is typical of the way emotions and mutual help are regarded in our organization. When members of my team talked about the dangerous young male patient, the psychiatrist did everything possible to relativize their feelings. His contribution was: 'It's okay to be afraid, but not too afraid, because you only make the situation even worse than it already is.'

Something is wrong somewhere

The day I return from my holiday, just as I have dragged my cases indoors, the telephone rings. Another suicide. The fourth in 18 months, the third in less than 6 months. This time it's a woman in her late twenties, who was found dead with a shoelace around her neck. From the moment her corpse is discovered, all kinds of doubts enter our minds: "This is impossible". We feel – without knowing precisely the basis for it – that there is more going on than we realize. In some cases you know that a suicide attempt is in the offing, but this was totally unexpected. The police arrive and carrying out their usual investigations in cases of violent death.

They find nothing suspicious and release the corpse. This is followed by 24 hours of speculation and suspicions.

Someone had seen a male co-patient nervously leave the young woman's room, just before her dead body was discovered. This patient had, for some time, had a somewhat half-hearted relationship with the suicide victim, who had broken it off two days before.

Twenty-four hours after the police had completed their investigations, the psychiatrist and the nursing manager decided to bring all the rumours to an end once and for all, by calling in the police for the second time. The police reopen the investigations, with some reluctance, and once again find nothing that might point to murder. The corpse also shows no signs of the patient having put up any kind of physical resistance. The patient whom we suspect is (therefore?) not questioned by the police.

After investigating the matter for three weeks, the police close their files. We, however, are left with the feeling that something is wrong somewhere. We find it very difficult to determine our attitude towards the 'suspect' patient, especially as he begins to act very strangely. He starts to use more drugs and his behaviour hardens.

Four months later he approaches me and says, literally, "I would like to discuss a very tricky question with you", and because I have already put my coat on to go to lunch, I ask him if it could not wait for an hour. "No", he says "it must be *now*". I take him to my office; we are hardly inside when he says: "I murdered G." I have no doubt at all that he is speaking the truth, and I feel myself turning white. Outwardly, however, I remain calm and say: "You understand of course that I have to do something about this. I will have to ring the police." Before telephoning the police, I give implicit instructions to my colleagues to keep a keen eye on him. There is a bomb sitting inside this young man: he could become psychotic, he could take his own life, or do some other awful thing. I can't help but feel a little surprised that despite the fact that he has murdered someone, I am still able to maintain a nursing relationship with him: what he has done disgusts me, I am angry with him, but I am still concerned about his welfare.

An hour and a half later, I am sitting in the car with the psychiatrist, on our way to the family in order to bring them the bad news. The psychiatrist leaves it to me to do the talking: "You are the head of the department, and furthermore the young man made his confession to you".

As we drive home after this, for me very difficult, discussion, we talk about this and that. Not about the murder, and not about his or my feelings. When I remind him of this later, he says it is quite normal, as if he is trying to say "that's the way it should be".

Help

From the moment the young man has made his confession to me, I start to sleep badly. The first night, I can't sleep at all, and toss and turn in bed. I have to face a barrage of images of what has happened in the department during the last two years. The most frequently recurring image is the moment that I and a colleague cut through the rope with which the man had hanged himself on the handgrip above his bed. Things do not improve very much after the first sleepless night. I sleep so little and so badly that after two weeks I am completely exhausted. I can't go on, and take sick leave.

Before that, however, I have succeeded in bringing the team together, and the management team has also invited itself to attend the discussion. It becomes clear during the discussion that something else is bothering the management team: the impending publicity. That is what they want to discuss with us.

The discussion which I had requested for the purpose of looking at "how are we coping now?" has been "stolen" from us by the management team. They would need half an hour, but it was in fact an hour. There is no more time for the real discussion. A more or less hostile atmosphere develops between us and the management; they place their problem above ours. Looking back, I should of course have refused to allow the management to take part in the discussion, but it's easy to talk after the event.

I talked regularly with my colleagues in those two weeks and I know that things are not only going badly with me, but that my colleagues are also finding it difficult. In the meantime, I have contacted the Psychotrauma Institute. "I am simply going to arrange something for myself," is how I explain my initiative to the management team. I tell them that I need help for the team and for myself, and will they pay for it? The management team agrees to my request. (They would later give themselves a pat on the back for having called in the help of the Psychotrauma Institute. My initiative, please note...)

At the moment the management gives its permission to accept help from the Institute mentioned, I am completely at the end of my tether and no longer able to take part in the group discussions. There is a total block in me. I have no choice but to take sick leave again and try, with the help of a psychologist, to get back on my feet again. There is no more possibility of participating in the group discussions under the guidance of the psychologist at the Psychotrauma Institute. During my absence, there is no one prepared to take over the care of my team. A week after me, and for the same reasons, one of my colleagues also "calls it a day". He places himself under the care of the same psychologist who is treating me.

The treatment I receive is not easy, but I do see signs that I am gradually finding my way out of the dark tunnel again. Two months after the onset of the treatment, I have progressed sufficiently to take on the most difficult assignment of the treatment so far: to return to my department three times within a two week period. I am dreading it. I make a considerable detour in driving to the hospital the first time, and with sweat on my brow I walk through the building. It is a strange experience to realize that I am actually not able to look more than two metres ahead of me – as if I am looking through a camera that has been focused in that way. It goes much better on the third occasion. I am able to say to myself then: "okay, this is it, this is where you have to come back to."

Shortly after my third visit to the department, I receive a telephone call from my boss saying he would like to talk to me. I am very pleased about this. After two difficult weeks of treatment, I have got so far that I actually want to talk with my colleague-team leaders and with my team. I want to hear from my team what they think about my breakdown, how they are feeling themselves, and what they think about my coming back. I have also discussed this plan with my psychologist.

My superior asks me how I am, and while I am telling him I notice that he is just not listening to me at all. When I have finished, he does not respond to anything I have said, but asks me: "How do you feel about coming back as team leader?" I don't quite understand the question. "I am the team leader, I have been ill and I am now coming back." He then says, however, that they have serious doubts about this: they have talked about me and they are asking themselves if I am a proper team leader.

When I ask him who are the people who have these doubts, it appears that it is not my team members, but my more senior colleagues. According to them, I often react too emotionally, involving my team members in my emotions. They regard me as a "softie", a product of the 1960s. This makes less impact on me, however, than something else which my boss tells me. During the course of discussions among the higher echelons of my colleagues, our psychiatrist has said that I have let my team down; that I became ill in the period that my team needed me most...

I am completely flabbergasted by this conversation. Now that I have found my way out of the pit, I fall to the bottom again. At the end of June – I have been ill for four months – I have a talk with the doctor at the local Mental Health Care Centre (MHCC). He advises to request a discussion with the management. I then try to contact the director of the hospital, but he is not available. Two days later – on my birthday! – he telephones me himself. He tells me that he has talked with my boss and that the board members have decided that they will not intervene in this matter and that I am allowed to communicate with them only through my boss. The director also says that an investigation of everything that has happened in my department during the past few years will be initiated. He adds that as team leader I fulfil a key position and that my functioning will, therefore, be critically assessed. I respond with "many ugly things have been said about me during my absence, and does this mean that this investigation could cost me my job?". His reply was: "On this point, I am unfortunately not able to assuage your fears."

A week later, my boss has a discussion with the Mental Health Care Centre, and what he says about me there is hardly flattering – on the contrary. The most unpleasant but at the same time most complimentary remark, is: 'Poor old Paul, he literally lays himself on the line between his team and the rest of the institute.'

The 'soul' has gone

We are now (July 1994) a month further and I am beginning to doubt more and more whether it would be wise to return to the hospital as team leader. Why? Because our supervising staff has no intention of providing care for its own personnel. Their view apparently is: "You get your salary, and in exchange for that you are expected to look after yourself."

Until recently, I used to think: "as long as it doesn't cost me my job". But I don't think that any more. If they want to throw me out, let them. I cannot function in an institution which cares so little for its own people. I have now been on sick leave for more than four months, and in that time none of my superiors has visited me or asked how I am. When I recently told the MHCC psychologist about this, he was speechless. No, I have no faith in the prevailing culture in our hospital. If I go back and someone else commits suicide, the same conflict will arise.

The stability and good atmosphere in our team, the relaxed spirit and the fun we used to have, have gone. The spirit has gone from our team. The team has been destroyed by everything that has happened and by the absence of any support. And still the hospital is saying out loud: "You should be able to take it, otherwise you are no good for this work." Or, as our psychiatrist said to me six months ago: "If I have two suicides on one day and I cannot take it, then there is no place for me here."

I will give you two more examples of how the management thinks it has the interests of the staff at heart. It was the practice in our team, following a suicide incident, to attend the cremation or funeral, or – if the family did not wish that – to hold our own memorial service. In this way, we ourselves could say our "good-byes" to the patient, and we usually prepared our own texts and poems for these services. I can remember very well the text I spoke during the service we attended for the young man who had hanged himself on the handgrip above his bed. A few days before the service, I was walking through a wood in which an enormous plague of caterpillars was destroying the trees. In my text, I compared the suicide with this caterpillar plague: you can see it happening before your very eyes but you can't do anything about it. You are completely helpless as a carer. But that is beside the point.

Just before the fourth suicide, we received a letter from the hospital director, informing us that he had serious doubts about our attending cremations and funerals for patients who had committed suicide. He explained it as follows: "If someone one-sidedly breaks a relationship, you just have to accept it." I was amazed at this. I remembered something a chaplain had once said to me: 'We cannot deny anyone the right to say "goodbye". Not the patient and not the nurse or other carers.'

Both my team members and I were deeply disappointed. The management were very concerned to write a letter to us, but none of them ever took the trouble to approach us and ask how we were doing!

We reached an impasse after this letter. The management wanted to lay a prohibition on us, but on this occasion we refused categorically to comply with it. Attending a service was the only opportunity we had of assessing our emotions in the wake of a death by suicide. It was necessary for our very survival. We have simply continued along our normal path. And there has been no further managerial reaction.

A second example of how the management thinks in terms of caring for its personnel: I received two telephone calls yesterday from colleagues working in my department who both said that their feelings were still not being taken seriously. During the evaluation investigation – which was attended by the management team, the psychiatrist and the head of the nursing care – one of my (telephone) colleagues had said: "If I have to treat a patient in the isolation cell, I feel even more insecure and afraid than I was before." No one responded. The second colleague had said: "I don't know whether I will be able to cope with yet another." And nothing was done with this comment either. Six months earlier, that same colleague had asked the management if he could work two days a week less. Forty hours in the week was too much for him. He later told me: "The only reason I asked for a cut in working hours at that time, was because I was afraid I would have a complete breakdown. I am working fewer hours now, but it is causing me financial difficulty."

I informed the management team of this. What I find so sad is that they do not take these kinds of "noises" seriously. And they don't want to. I can't take this any more. If this is the way it has to be, then I am going to stop.'

8 'Please help me make it through the night'

Raymonda's story

'I decided, after a great deal of hesitation, to put my story on paper because I would very much like to see a book published on the subject of traumatic events in the nursing field. I have no doubt at all that it will be a relief for many to know that attention is at last being focused on their feelings and emotions, and that they can finally express things that are so often ignored in nursing institutions.

Something happens during your working day which has extremely far-reaching effects. If you are lucky, you find your colleagues are sympathetic and encouraging in the first few days, but all too soon the air buzzes with the "life goes on" cliche, and you certainly dare not say anything more, or tell your story again, because it soon gets labelled as "whining".

What happened

It is 11 o'clock on Tuesday evening, 4th September 1991. I am on night duty with M, a fully qualified Registered General Nurse (RGN). Having taken over from the evening shift, we begin our first bed round. We visit all the patients. It is our sixth night in a row and we decide first of all to have a drink. We know all the patients and nothing significant had happened during the evening shift.

We talk together about my having to write my thesis and M explains what happens during the final oral test. I am half way through my third year of training and will be taking my finals in a few months' time as well as submitting my final essay. This is a tense period, knowing that after seven years of hard grind I will have achieved my RGN diploma.

M says she is very satisfied with my work and that she feels I am quite capable of running a team on my own. (The ward has two teams – the first, the surgery team with twelve beds; the second the rehabilitation team with ten beds. During the other shifts I always work in team one, and my task this time is thus to look after and monitor the patients on the surgical team.)

It is now midnight. We each go to our own teams to consult the patient files and to record the fluid levels. While I am doing this, I notice that Mr T is sitting by the window. He is a patient on Ward 1 who had undergone an aorta-bifurcation four days previously. He was transferred from intensive care today. He has two drains, a bladder catheter and a jugular catheter to which the drip is attached.

I walk over to Mr T and ask him if there is anything wrong, and after a short chat I help him back to bed. When I leave the room, I am struck by the fact that he has carefully detached all the equipment from his bed and laid it neatly on the table by the window.

I am just finishing the paperwork when there is a call that someone on Ward 1 has rung the bell, and I go there immediately. The patient opposite Mr T has pressed the bell because Mr T is trying to get out of bed again. I thank the patient for warning me and walk towards Mr T's bed.

I ask him what the matter is and he answers that there is nothing wrong, but that he just wants to sit next to his bed. I say that it is already very late and that in the darkness he is likely to fall over things in his path. He understands the situation perfectly and crawls back into bed. I ask him if he would like anything to help him sleep, but he does not. I wish him 'good night' and leave the room.

M has by this time also completed her work. We discuss Mr T and decide that we will both look in on him at regular intervals. We continue with our normal night work duties and because I am ultimately responsible for Mr T, I visit his bedside practically every quarter of an hour, over and above the normal supervisory visits. And he is still awake, every time, returning to his seat by the window several times during the night.

I get a strange feeling about this man, not because he is confused or restless, but rather because he is so calm and acquiescent…and he remains so for the rest of the night.

M also makes frequent visits to Mr T's bedside to see how he is, and in order to give me a chance to get on with my other jobs. At approximately 2.30 in the morning we have both completed our work and spend the rest of the night in the staff coffee room; you enter it via the ward kitchen and you, therefore, have no direct view of the ward, except through the corridor windows.

The night proceeds without any further interruptions. We each take it in turn to check on Mr T; he is still 'busy', but there is nothing disturbing about him.

At the 5.45 am check, Mr T has finally fallen asleep. We decide not to make such frequent checks because we are afraid of waking him if we come too close to his bedside.

The telephone rings at 6.15 am and our first reaction is to expect an emergency admission, but a colleague (an RGN) announces her arrival for day duty. Because there is a minimum number of staff on duty and now one student nurse will be running the first team alone, we decide to begin our morning round (pulse and temperature taking, bedpans and cups of tea) earlier than usual so that we can wash as many patients as possible before we leave. Normally speaking, we never begin washing the patients so early, because everybody is so against it, on principle.

We drink another cup of tea quickly and enter the ward to begin our work. When we leave the kitchen at 6.20 am, we see a half-full drain pot at the entrance to the ward. We glance at each other and run to Ward 1. M walks via a narrow corridor into the sluice (the room where the bedpans are stored and cleaned). I walk straight through to the corridor that leads to Ward 1 and suddenly M calls my name. I stiffen almost. In a reflex movement, I open the bathroom door and come face to face with Mr T. We look at each other, but he doesn't see me. He is more or less hanging on the wc – you could hardly call it sitting. He is naked and is covered with blood, with waves of blood streaming from his neck. I call for M.

Walking through the pools of blood, I have to take hold of myself, as I feel myself engulfed in a wave of panic. We lay Mr T on the bathroom floor and M places him in a stable position on his side and squeezes the cut end of the jugular catheter in order to prevent any further blood loss.

I run quickly to the telephone and dial the alarm number and the night charge nurse. I then race to the other ward to get the lifepack; I meet another nurse there and hastily tell her what is going on. She immediately returns with me to the bathroom in case she can be of any help.

It feels like forever before the reanimation team arrives and before I am back with M. In fact, I was hardly back before they arrived. I quickly close the door of Ward 1 so that the other patients will not see what is happening.

I will never forget the look on everyone's faces (the reanimation team and the night sisters). One of the sisters gave us a thorough telling-off, without knowing exactly what had happened. Why had we let such a thing happen, we should have kept a better eye on the patient, we had obviously spent the whole night in the coffee room etc., etc.

Mr T's heart beat suddenly stops, and M and I hold our breath and our hearts stop beating too. We hope that the reanimation will succeed, but after a long effort, the reanimation team has to give up the fight. The patient has lost too much blood. "He is dead" runs through my body like a knife. The reanimation team gather up their equipment and disappear. The duty surgeon (called by one of the sisters) says, more blaming than asking: "How could you both let such a thing happen?", adding under his breath "And that's what you call Registered General Nurses."

M and I lift Mr T onto his bed, which I have already brought from the ward. I notice too that the other patients are watching me intently. For fear that they will start asking questions, I pretend I haven't noticed their looks.

We push the bed to the examination room and stand beside it numb and speechless. One of the night charge nurses comes into the room and growls that we are going to find ourselves in serious trouble, because she is going to report the matter.

I start to swear deep inside. M cries and walks along the corridor – ostensibly to collect the box containing the items required to prepare a patient for the mortuary, but I know that she is trying to hide her sorrow. I also feel pangs of anger, sorrow and pain, but I can't express them. I say to myself 'Don't cry – not now, not here'. I pull flannels from the cupboard and I drop half of them on the floor.

But what must I do? Mr T is covered in blood. It really doesn't make much difference, I might as well make a start. I wonder what is keeping M so long. I am afraid, very afraid. I start the washing procedure any way.

When M finally comes, she is still crying and she asks me where I had begun the washing whereupon, to my utter surprise, I say I had begun by the toes. We do the work like robots and in silence. Apart from a muted sob now and again, there is an icy silence.

When we are nearly finished, one of the night sisters arrives (having said nothing all the time). She says she has cleaned the sluice and the bathroom as well as possible. The enormous quantity of blood surprised her. Without further ado and without our thanking her for her help, she departs again. The other night charge nurse left quite some time ago.

Whilst we are tidying our things, we hear the day duty staff arriving on the ward. We go to the kitchen as quickly as possible, because we still have to do the morning patient round. In the meantime, I have put my emotions on 'non-active' and automatically put the kettle on for a cup of tea.

One of the day duty colleagues comes over to us – she has already noticed that all is not well. When she asks M what has happened, M breaks down. They go to the coffee room together and I am left alone. I feel very lonely all of a sudden and feel I have been abandoned. I get the feeling that a student nurse is not considered to be a full member of the ward staff.

Before I even have the chance of starting on the morning patient round, the other day staff arrive. I am ashamed of my emotions and I forbid myself to let even one tear fall. What I can't hide, however, is my flushed face and the fact that my whole body is trembling.

M relates the whole story. I feel so guilty and dare not look at anyone. I am afraid to meet their eyes. One of the day staff (a team leader) suddenly asks if anything else of importance has happened tonight. I can hardly believe my ears. I rise to my feet in a flash and make a rough grab for my bag. M and I exchange glances – too tired to say anything at all. And to make matters even worse, the team leader then adds "Sleep well". I am furious and almost let fly a flood of abuse, but manage to check myself in time.

In order to avoid an escalation of the situation, M and I make a hasty retreat. We meet the duty surgeon in the corridor. Mr T's family has been informed; unfortunately, we had forgotten them completely. I ask the surgeon to pass on the information to the day duty staff.

In the changing room I notice that I too am covered in blood. There are large stains on my uniform and shoes and M's uniform is also not entirely white. I feel dirty and hope that we will not meet anyone on our way to the car park. There is, in fact, just one hasty handshake. What, after all, can you say at such a moment?

Passages from my diary

Wednesday, 5 September 1991, 11.00 hours

Help! I let a patient die this morning. Why didn't I check him more often? It's my fault. He was my patient. How can I answer for this?

I have 'phoned my best friend J, but she is out. Whenever I close my eyes I see the patient before me. It is like a film in slow motion. I am hit by every kind of emotion, but am unable to vent them. Oh God, help me please!

*It is one o'clock in the afternoon, and I still haven't slept. I have
told my mother. She was very upset, but tried to comfort me. But no
one can lessen my sorrow. How is M managing? I am unable to reach
her. Did it really happen? Tell me it was just a nightmare. Please
wake me and tell me that it is not true! I have one more night shift. I
want to stay at home but, for the sake of the patients and staff, I can't
do that. I hope M will come too. Oh God, I am so afraid of going
back to the ward, to the patients. Am I fit for this work? Please, help
me make it through the night!*

Thursday, 6 September, 10.00 hours

*M is there too, thank goodness. On the way to the hospital, my
nerves gripped my whole body. The police have visited the ward –
they have to investigate what caused Mr T's death. They suspect that
he committed suicide. They found his small gold scissors in the sluice
and suspect that he used his own scissors on purpose. There were, after
all, other scissors in the bandage trays. The fact that Mr. T had cut
all the tubes whilst he was in the sluice and not on the ward and that
he then went to sit in the bathroom, reinforces the police's suspicion
that it was a deliberate act.*

*According to Mr. T's wife, he often had periods of depression, and
on the evening prior to his death, she had heard a nurse say to him
that he mustn't do anything silly.*

*M said that during one of her checks, Mr T had thanked her for
her excellent care. We are often thanked in our work, but perhaps this
should have been an indicator for us.*

*M and I talked little this evening. We just did our work and
nothing more. I think we were really trying to kid each other, for fear
of losing control of our emotions.*

*We had to report to the head of the Personnel Department at 8 am.
We have written our whole story. I felt just like a small child being
reprimanded, because I had done something naughty. Apparently, one
of the night charge nurses had reported the incident.*

*Fortunately, I have a few days off. Every time I walked past the
bathroom, I saw it all again before my eyes. Will this anxiety ever go
away? I am so tired but dare not sleep.*

Friday, 7 September 1991, 22.00 hrs.

Interests? No, life just goes on. It is allowed to cry a little (at least, if you can). But certainly not too long. I am so nervous. Have still not slept. Where do I go from here?

Monday, 10 September 1991, 12.00 hrs.

It's Monday again, and I hoped this day would never come. I have to start work again this afternoon. Night duty with M.

I didn't sleep again last night. I dare not. I am afraid of my colleagues. The autopsy report will be issued at 16.00 hours. M and I have to present ourselves again.

I want to report sick, but I know I can't. I will try to rest for a while, and perhaps I will feel a little better.

It is 13.00 hours. What is happening to me? I dozed off for a while. Dreamt that I was sentenced by a judge. I had to go to prison, because I had committed murder. Please don't let it be true!

Tuesday, 11 September 1991, 04.00 hrs.

It has been a busy shift. Am so unsure of myself. I jump at every sound and then go and investigate it. The autopsy concludes the Mr T died as a result of the accident. We now have to wait and see whether the family is going to file an official complaint with the police.

I found the scissors this afternoon, and put them with the aid of tweezers into an envelope. On no account must my fingerprints be on them. I have put it in a good hiding place, because it is official evidence. Am I really going mad?

Able to talk with J at last. She had some idea of what had happened, but not about who had been directly involved. I am so happy I have her. She knows what to do, or what not to do. We talked for four hours and I know there will be many more nightime discussions like this.

How did I get on after that?

I reported sick a week later because I couldn't take the pressure any more. The biggest blow for me was the enormous lack of understanding among the people around me. I certainly expected a more professional attitude from my colleagues. Suddenly they seem unaware of concepts such as empathy and support in a mourning process.

I still keep being told that life must go on, but that was, and is, not true for me. Thanks to support from J, I managed to complete my training successfully – by the skin of my teeth, however, and thanks to the sick leave I was able to take. J dragged, kicked (figuratively speaking) and pulled me through it. She helped me gather my strength together every morning, just to get up and get myself to work. We often went together, J bringing me right up to the ward. We have often stood together outside the bathroom and entered it hand in hand. She was often very hard on me, but wonderful nonetheless!

Now that we are no longer living together (we used to share a student flat in the same unit), I miss her more and more. We telephone each other often, but a conversation face to face is so much better.

It all happened more than eighteen months ago, and I never thought I would survive it. Perhaps you are thinking "strange that this story is written in the present tense", but it still plays an important role in my daily life. And I still have nightmares.

Perhaps putting it down on paper is a kind of therapy in itself for me, and even if it doesn't work, it might perhaps be of interest to others.

Whether or not it changes anything for me, I cannot say. I am still nursing in the same hospital. I have, therefore, been on sick leave for more than eight months because of chronic eczema. My dermatologist says that the eczema, which began in December 1991, is caused by enormous stress. Whatever – I can put it another way, of course: i.e. that the allergy itself has been there for some time, but has only now erupted because of the stress. I am being treated with several ointments at the moment, and go under the PUVA twice a week – with, alas, little effect so far. I have even bought new shoes which have no chrome parts on them, but if they don't have the desired effect, I will have to quit my profession. I feel this as punishment for what happened.'

9 'Hetty dear, you will never have to be a party to it again'

Hetty's story

'Between 1977 and 1980, I worked as a night sister in a fairly large hospital in the west of the country. I was responsible for the Obstetrics, Maternity and Gynaecology departments. My work was actually concentrated on the delivery rooms, i.e. Obstetrics. This is the department where besides the Outpatients, clinical premature deliveries also took place. The babies born between the 16th and 28th weeks of gestation, were very frail and most of them died. Babies born after the 28th week of the pregnancy usually survived, although often only after pulling out all the stops.

There was a strong sense of team spirit between the doctors and nursing staff surrounding the births of these babies: everyone and everything was focused on allowing this new life to be born under the best possible conditions.

Our work had something schizophrenic about it sometimes, in that in the clinical delivery room everything possible was being done to save a pregnancy, whilst in another room further down the corridor a pregnancy was being terminated. Obstetrics was of course the department where, usually on social indications, pregnancies were terminated well beyond the abortion stage; in contrast to abortion, we were concerned here with women sixteen weeks or more into their pregnancies. Whilst fierce political discussions were going on about the moral and ethical aspects of such pregnancy terminations, women came to the hospital for them from every corner of the country.

Staff was minimal at nights. I usually worked with a second or third year student nurse, and also on occasions with nurses doing their obstetric nursing training. The rule was that student nurses were not involved in treating women undergoing a pregnancy termination – or in our jargon, a late abortion. This meant that in such cases I was the only qualified nurse available.

Having sketched the general atmosphere, I will now move on to the incident which can still reduce me to tears even after so many years. The young woman in my story had come to our hospital for a pregnancy termination. She was given the appropriate injection of ureum, a substance which kills the fetus (probably to justify what we were doing, both to ourselves and others, we used the term fetus, although we were in fact dealing with a very tiny baby, a human being complete and intact). When the ureum had done its work, the woman received a drip to stimulate the contractions. Despite this, however, the delivery as such, took some time, as is often the case.

The torso of a tiny baby

When I go on night duty, the baby has still not come. The patient is very restless. She knows, just as I do, that in such an early stage of a pregnancy, the child can lie in the womb in all kinds of positions: head down, breech or transverse.

Insofar as my other tasks allow, I try to be with the patient as much as possible. I support and help her as much as I can; I help her to change her lying position, I freshen her up, help her with breathing exercises, administer the prescribed painkillers and sedating medicines to her, sit next to her and try to talk with her. Despite the breathing exercises and the medication, I see no progress and the patient remains restless. I telephone the junior gynaecologist on duty, and he says "surely you can cope with this situation on your own". That is his way of saying he is not prepared to come.

I have no choice but to return to my patient, and she is still restless. I still feel very uneasy about the situation. Something is wrong, but what? There was no indication that the baby was in the breech position when I performed the vaginal examination. My unease was so great at a certain moment, that I decided to ring the doctor again. This time, I am determined: "You must come now". That worked, and he promised to come.

I go back to the patient, and while she and I are waiting for the doctor to arrive, the baby's lower body emerges. A breech baby. I try to support the mother as much as possible ("the doctor will soon be here") and encourage her to hang on tight. When the doctor finally arrives, he begins to pull the baby's body with one hand, with his other hand on the patient's tummy in order to hold the baby's head. There seems to be no end to all the pulling and heaving. We are not having any success, and as time goes by, the doctor's handling of mother and child becomes steadily rougher and more desperate. Finally, he succeeds in releasing the baby from the womb...without its head.

The doctor hands the headless body to me, and I lay it in a large basin. At his request, I go to collect some forceps with which he draws the baby's head from the womb. His work done, he removes his surgical gloves, puts them on the bed and departs without saying a word to either the patient or to me.

I proceed as is expected of me. I do what I must for the child and the patient, and I tidy everything up. Only when the new team comes on duty, can I say anything about what happened that night...in medical terms.

I have had nightmarish dreams ever since. I feel caught in a very tight spot. I don't know where the dreams come from. I do not relate them to this awful incident.

I say nothing about it for years. There is nothing special or abnormal about it. In those days, these things were not talked about, and in consequence it never occurs to me to talk about it.

Things changed, however, when in the mid-1980s, I saw Polanski's film of 'Macbeth'. At the end of the film, all kinds of people are beheaded, and the heads are placed on swords and exhibited on the walls of the castle. I reacted with such intensity to these images that a friend who was with me kept asking me about it. And for the first time I talk about the incident that had taken place whilst I was on night duty all those years ago.

During this conversation it becomes apparent that a picture has remained glued to the night-side of my retina: the body of a tiny baby, badly mauled and broken, firstly as a result of the ureum, and then as a result of rough manipulation by the doctor; a doctor who removes his gloves, leaves them on the bed, and departs without a word.

The nightmares cease after this talk.

Epilogue

In putting this experience to paper, I noticed that there were still many more tears to be shed, in fact they tumbled like a waterfall down my cheeks. And during the writing itself, I felt a tightness in my chest. Before I was actually able to write my story, I first of all felt compelled to tell two of my closest friends about it. On the second occasion especially, I was able to have a really good cry and feel the intense distress of tearing a tiny baby torso to pieces like that. What I found particularly comforting were the words of my friend: "Dear Hetty, you will never have to be a party to it again.'"

Part 2

Theory

Chapter 1

Very Dramatic Incidents and Psychotrauma

Introduction

A nurse: 'A young boy of seven years had been severely bitten by a pitbull terrier, and died later as a result of his wounds. The ambulance had called in advance for reanimation following excessive loss of blood and wounds to the face and neck. The child was brought into the hospital and immediately put on reanimation; he also had extremely severe mutilations to his face and neck. It was decided an hour later to stop the reanimation treatment because the child's heartbeat could not be restored and his neck was probably broken as well. This all made a very deep impression on me, partly because the child had also been so badly mutilated. I later discussed the case with my colleagues who were also involved in the child's initial treatment as well as with the ambulance personnel, but the image of that little boy remained in my mind and I had many a sleepless night because of it.'

Nurses and nursing assistants (from this point on, I will use only the term 'nurses' to mean both nurses and nursing assistants) belong to a group which carries a high risk of being confronted with extreme and deeply emotional events. What makes nursing different from other professions is that the people with whom they are most directly involved are so dependent on them for the most important aspect of their lives: their health. And the question of health – meaning everything we meet between life and death, between complete independence and total dependence – is always highly emotive. We see this very clearly when people who, in normal circumstances, appear to have their emotions perfectly under control, but who as patients – when confronted by serious disorders or life-threatening illnesses – suddenly become frail and vulnerable.

Nurses are frequently faced in their daily lives with a side of life which others not involved in health care only see very occasionally; namely suffering, physical and mental deterioration, and death. For health workers, these moments which border on life itself, are a daily reality. Many nurses encounter, in the space of a few years, more moments of deep emotion than an 'ordinary' person will meet in a whole lifetime, and the same is even more true of ambulance workers who can come face-to-face with more distress and pain in a few months than the average 'lay' person in a full life-span.

A multi-form phenomenon

'When, as an ambulance nurse you have to deal with someone who has fallen under the wheels of a train and you have two boots in your hand with the man's lower legs still in them, it's an image that remains with you for years. But you just have to go on.'

Ambulance nurses stand in the forefront of the health care services and they run a higher risk of having to do their work under extremely dramatic and disturbing conditions. They are often the first on the scene of all kinds of human dramas, such as traffic accidents, burns, stabbings, drownings and other human catastrophes. In line with other front-line care workers, such as police officers and firemen, ambulance personnel dread most of all having to deal with the aftermath of accidents involving children. An ambulance nurse:

'Some time ago, I was called out to reanimate a baby of a few months old. When we arrived and entered the bedroom, the family doctor was already there, and reanimation was no longer possible. We saw a baby lying in its cot, with its face already markedly blue in colour: dead. He had wormed his way under the duvet to the foot of the bed, and his sleeping bag then prevented his getting back from under the duvet, and as a result he suffocated. When you see something like that, it hits you very hard. Even if you have done this work for twelve years or more, as I have. But you have to do your work and the coping comes later, or so you think; if you are lucky, you are able to talk about it at home or with your colleagues. I am extremely thankful that our twin boys have passed the "cot death" age.'

The sight of a badly burned or mutilated child is something that even the most experienced of ambulance personnel never gets used to, or remains unmoved by. Accidents in which they can be of no help, being able to do nothing but simply watch the suffering as the victim's life ebbs away – such as someone being crushed and the fire brigade arriving later than the ambulance – remain imprinted in their minds for all time.

In December 1992, Ravenscraft (1994) investigated stress levels (with the help of a questionnaire) in 1420 members of London's ambulance service. The response was 39 per cent, and the study showed that the majority (52%) were suffering a high degree of stress. Even more remarkable was that 15 per cent of the ambulance nurses were suffering from the Post Traumatic Stress Syndrome (PTSD), i.e. a combination of various stress symptoms (see p.77 for definition). The study also revealed that the stress symptoms were not necessarily the result of their being involved in large-scale human catastrophes, but had much more to do with difficult, routine, 999 telephone calls, such as a child badly injured in a car crash.

The victims taken by the ambulances to the hospitals, are admitted first of all to the Accident and Emergency Department, and it is the nurses working there who constitute the second group of carers regularly put to the test in terms of coping with human dramas and stress. A nurse:

'At 17.00 hours we received warning of the arrival of a multi-trauma: various rib fractures, brain damage and shock. It was a young man of 27. Specialists, housemen, X-ray staff and operating theatre personnel were on hand. The patient's condition worsened during the CT-scanning. Reanimation was started – and it was a horrible sensation to feel the patient's ribs moving under my hands – but he died. Death having been pronounced, the medical team left. Pressure of work in other departments meant that colleagues could not come to help me, and I was left alone with the dead man. The family had to be received, the body had to be prepared, and I was the one who had to confront the family with the situation; I felt I had to cope with everything alone. A dreadful situation, terrible images, which have stayed in my mind for a long time. There was no discussion of the situation, either on the evening itself with the other staff involved, nor the following day with the head of the department!'

Following the initial First Aid care, the baton of human misery is often passed on to the nurses in the operating rooms and the Intensive Care (IC) units. If, as an IC nurse, you have been fighting for a patient's life for days or even weeks, and you have built up a relationship with the patient and have the feeling that you have also become part of the family, it can be devastating when you and your patient ultimately lose the battle.

Nurses in other hospital departments, nursing homes, homes for the elderly, or in the community, may not usually be so involved in dramas of such emotional intensity, but they too are confronted with a considerable degree of human suffering. Of all health care workers, it is the nursing staff who are most in the firing line, as it were, and they cannot cut themselves off completely from their patient's emotions. Indeed, they must not. Nursing and caring are only really possible if those involved are open to people expressing what they actually feel, such as vulnerability, suffering, guilt feelings and so forth.

Finding an answer when the patient asks something, communicating with him, showing empathy with him – are all impossible if care workers close the door on their own personal emotions. If they do not want to act in a robot-like way or from a distance, but want to give themselves, heart and soul, to the nursing task, then they will *have* to listen and respond to their own emotions. The risk is that every time a nurse enters the emotional world of the patient, she too will feel a high degree of emotional pain. Imagine the sorrow felt by a nurse at the death of a patient she has nursed with care and devotion for a long time. For confirmation of this, we only have to listen to the stories of nurses on the cancer wards.

The Jewish American writer, Philip Roth, who in his latest (semi-autobiographical) book has succeeded in creating a subtle mixture of fiction and reality, portrays a nurse named Jinx who breaks down as a result of her work on the Oncology Department, as a minor character in his book. *Operation Shylock* (1993).

> "'I got drawn into people's suffering," she said. "I couldn't help it. If they cry, I hold their hand. I hug them – If they cry, I cry. I hug them, they hug me – to me there's no way not to. It's like you're their saviour. Jinx could do no wrong. But I can't be their savior. And that got me after a while.'"

When she has to take care of a young female patient, it all becomes too much for her.

> "'But she was a woman my age – so young, so young. She had cancer *everywhere*. And she was in so much pain. She was in *so* much pain. Mr. Roth, a *terrific* amount of pain. (…) She was going to die anyway, she was ready to die, but she died on me. I killed her. Her skin was beautiful. You know? She was a waitress. A good person. An outgoing person. She told me she wanted six children. But I gave her morphine and she died. I went berserk. I went to the bathroom and went hysterical.'"

The staff nurse, who wants to do the best she can for her, then arranges her transfer to the surgical ward. "There's always hope on the surgical floor."

The risk of being shaken by events is greater on one ward than another, although there is virtually nowhere in nursing where dramas of some kind are not lurking just around the corner. Disturbing events can take place, even on a maternity ward. The case of a child with spina bifida or hydrocephalus, for instance, not only shatters the golden dreams of the parents, but it also constitutes a threat to the psychological wellbeing of the nursing staff.

Apart from such confrontations with human suffering, there is yet another important reason why nurses can develop severe psychic problems in the course of their work: this is the incidence of real or imagined nursing errors, especially if they result in permanent damage, a handicap or death. Even cases of error which have no lasting effects can reduce a nurse to a state of emotional turmoil. One nurse told me, for instance, that she had considered giving up her profession for a long time, because she had forgotten to close an incubator, with a baby in it, during her training. She could think of nothing else for weeks and the image of a falling baby became almost an obsession with her.

Another example of the dramatic incidents category in nursing is patient/client violence, which until fairly recently was a strictly taboo subject in the nursing world. It was not so much the violence itself which was difficult to talk about, but more particularly the anxiety felt by nurses in the face, and aftermath, of physical violence against them. Those highest on the risk-ladder are the professionals working with psychiatric patients. Psychiatry and violence have gone hand in hand for centuries. This is illustrated in the following quote from the former international footballer Jan Wouters (Visser 1994):

> 'My father was a house painter and maintenance mechanic in the psychiatric institution in the Agnietenstraat (in Utrecht, HB). I visited the place sometimes and found it very frightening. There were deeply disturbed and depressive people there. My father once told me that he had to restrain patients who were busy destroying everything in sight or throwing tiles from the roof. I was always afraid when I went there, but that feeling lessened in the course of time.'

Patient assault has become something of a *hot item* among psychiatric nursing personnel in the last few years. Research studies into physical assault follow each other in quick succession from the end of the 1980s onwards and there is no consensus in their findings. They do, however, make it quite clear that physical violence in psychiatry is frequent. Bijl and Lemmens (1993) report that every year approximately 75 per cent of all psychiatric nurses have to deal with violent patients. In the study carried out by Van de Velde and Herpers (1994), this figure even reached 85 per cent; according to these researchers, one in ten psychiatric nurses would be confronted by aggression every month, and of these 40 per cent would suffer injury of some kind. An American study (1989) in a forensic psychiatric setting revealed a lower incidence of physical injury; it produced an annual figure of 16 out of every 100 nurses suffering injury. The main difference between the latter study and the former three lies primarily in how people define 'violence' and 'physical injury'. A bruise on the arm as a result of it being squeezed is of quite a different order from being stabbed in the stomach. Dekker and Iping (1995) found in their study that serious incidents of violence were relatively infrequent, namely once a year per department. When aggression towards the nurse is given full rein, and certainly when a physical assault results in (lasting) physical damage, the nurse's world can change in a flash, both literally and figuratively speaking. The feeling of being safe, without which practically no one can function well, is destroyed. Another nurse writes:

'Years ago I was threatened with a knife by a psychotic patient nearing the end of her pregnancy. We were in a very small kitchen and she was standing just in front of me. She was blocking the doorway and I could not get out. I'll never survive this, I thought. But I felt an enormous will to survive nonetheless. I can't remember what I said to her at the time, but I was apparently able to persuade her to lay down the knife. Nothing happened ultimately, but it has troubled me ever since, and I have not talked about it.'

Most of the publications on the subject of violence against nursing staff concern incidents in the psychiatric field. It would be a mistake, however, to think that nurses working in other kinds of caring units, are not equally at risk of being assaulted at some time.

Assaults can occur in a variety of in-patient and out-patient settings. Nurses in paediatric units, in homes for the mentally handicapped and general hospitals, for instance, can all become the victims of violence.

The English *Nursing Times*, invited its readers to complete a questionnaire about their experiences of being assaulted by patients, and more than 500 nurses responded. Physical assault was defined as 'any physical contact by a patient or client that results in the feeling of being personally threatened'. The nurses were employed in various work settings, almost 75 per cent in hospitals, and the remaining 25 per cent in a community setting; a third were working with mental health patients. More than 50 per cent of the respondents indicated that they had been assaulted between one and nine times in their career (see Table 1.1). Just 8 per cent, that is, less than 1 in 10, indicated they had never in their career been assaulted.

Table 1.1: Assault experience of survey respondents (n=554)

Assault in current post %		Assault in career %		Most recent assault %	
None	31	None	8	1 month	26
1–3	33	1–3	30	1–3 months	18
4–9	19	4–9	27	4–6 months	10
10–15	6	10–15	12	7–12 months	12
> 15	11	> 15	22	> 12 months	

Note: All percentages have been rounded up
From: *Nursing Times*, volume 89, no. 48, 1993

In Western society, there has been a growing trend in the last decade towards more frequent violence, and at the same time we also see that assaultive behaviour is becoming more and more brutal. Nurses also are having to deal increasingly with more extreme types of violence.

A nurse working in an Emergency and Accident department describes how she was once threatened by a patient wielding a pistol (!) at her:

'I can recall the situation very clearly. The patient concerned came complaining of pain in the ribs. He had to wait four minutes. This was obviously too long for him, because he suddenly produced a pistol. He then threatened me, the porter and two fellow-nurses with it. By talking with the patient, I was finally able to persuade him to put his pistol down, and I could telephone the police.'

Nurses employed in nursing homes and homes for the aged are also having to face the increasing threat of being confronted by intruders.

'Last year, I was also the victim of a confrontation with someone breaking into the nursing home where I work in the evenings as a nursing assistant. I had caught the man "red handed". That, and the thought of what could have happened, has made me very uneasy and insecure in my work ever since. In the weeks immediately following the event, I received plenty of support from my employer and my colleagues. But after that, they soon forgot about it. Fortunately, the directors of the nursing home have since then instituted a number of preventive measures, including cameras at all entrances and exits, better lighting and alarm buttons on the call-up bleepers. But my feeling of safety has been destroyed for all time. And, unfortunately, I seldom discuss it with others. It is expected that I too will have forgotten about it, one year on.'

In community nursing too, a growing number of cases of threatening behaviour and robberies are being reported. Community nurse, Anny L, had a similar frightening experience:

'When, at the end of my evening shift, I was about to close the health centre door, I suddenly felt a hand on my shoulder. I turned round and saw a man with a knife in his hand. He wanted money, he said. I was too shocked to do or say anything. He began to body-search me but found nothing. Then he saw my wedding ring and pointed his knife towards my fingers. I gave him a short, sharp kick and slid into the building. I was well counselled (by our psychologist) but, even after two years, I still dread the evening shift. Six months after this incident, I took sick-leave for four months. And then suddenly I was able to shed my fear.'

Psychiatric patient stabs nurse

Noordwijkerhout – Last Monday, a 52-year-old psychiatric nurse in the Langeveld Psychiatric Centre in Noordwijkerhout, was stabbed in the back by a patient wielding a knife. The nurse was taken to the Academic hospital in Leiden and is now out of danger.

The nurse had worked for the last eight years in the outpatients department in the Bavo location in Noordwijkerhout, where his task was to administer medication to chronic psychiatric patients. The 39-year-old patient arrived on Monday morning for his weekly injection. While the nurse was preparing the hypodermic syringe, the patient, for no apparent reason, grasped his penknife and stabbed the nurse in the ribs. Personnel in the office nearby were able to overpower the patient and he was taken into police custody. The patient had been living in a four-person unit in the closed section at Langeveld. According to Langeveld's spokes-woman, K. Pijnenburg, it is not possible to prevent such incidents entirely. 'There are no checks on what patients carry with them', she says. 'In this case, the nurse had known the patient for eight years and had had no reason to fear any violence. There had been very few such incidents during that time in the outpatient depart-ment.' According to the spokeswoman, both personnel and pa-tients have been gravely shocked by this incident.' (*Verpleegkunde Nieuws*, no. 20, 29–9–1994, p. 5)

Nurses, especially those working in institutions where patients undergo long-term nursing care, can also become the victims of violence directed at them from the patients' own relatives and other visitors. This type of assault – which, as far as I know, has seldom been discussed in the literature – occurs most frequently in nursing homes. The motive behind the violence is most often a feeling of dissatisfaction about the nursing care itself (Vinton and Mazza 1994). This phenomenon also occurs, although to a lesser degree, in psychiatric centres, and is usually provoked by a close relative's strong objection to his relative being admitted for psychiatric treatment; his feelings run so high that he will stop at nothing in his efforts to turn the situation around.

Suicide, or – more frequently – the threat of suicide, can also be a very disturbing experience for those close to the perpetrator. When a patient succeeds in suiciding in a psychiatric hospital or centre, it will be the nurse who has had the closest contact with the patient, and will be most affected by it, particularly if the patient had already given warning of his/her intentions. The lesser shocks among nurses can also coincide with distressing events in their personal lives, such as the death of a parent, divorce, or one of their own children becoming seriously ill. Work conflicts with heads of departments or colleagues can also contribute to a nurse's breakdown in the face of a serious incident in the medical field.

Most nurses are female and her uniform is no guarantee of protection against sexual harassment. In fact, the contrary would seem to be true. In order to help a patient or client, she has to come physically close to him. Nursing care also entails touching erogenous areas of the body, which sometimes places not only the client, but the nurse herself, in an extremely vulnerable position: when someone is in close proximity to another, there is always a danger that one will make subtle or explicit sexual approaches to the other. Such as the client who removed the pubic hair around his penis and said to the community nurse whilst she was washing him: 'Now I can feel you better.'

The mildest form of sexual approach comes from clients who, because of their age, weak condition or disability, are physically weaker than the nurse. These patients can, nonetheless, create extremely uncomfortable situations for nurses.

Mr Jones, 84 years old, is in the early stages of dementia. He has been a heavy drinker for many years and after a few drinks he invariably begins to talk about sex. His regular nurse for the last three years, Clare, never responds. 'Those words and that type of language are not directed to me personally, so they don't bother me', she reasons. It usually stops if she doesn't react.

But one Sunday, Clare finds Mr Jones masturbating naked on the floor. She gets quite a shock, goes immediately to the kitchen and makes clattering noises with cups, in the hope that he will realize she is there. When he fails to stop, however, she walks toward to him and says: 'Mr Jones, you will catch a cold'. He tries to pull her towards him. She holds him at bay with the words: 'No, that is not what I come for, get yourself dressed' and she throws his pyjamas to him.

Clare gets him into his pyjamas, without washing him and, having prepared sandwiches and coffee for him, she leaves. Once in the car, however, she finds herself shaking from the shock, and because there is no one in the office at the weekend, she decides to go home before going on to the next client. She has to visit Mr Jones again in the afternoon, and he starts all over again. She says: 'Now you had better listen to me carefully. We can't work like this, and if we decide not to come any more, you will have to go to a nursing home.' The look in his eyes tells her that he understands, but whilst she is washing him he grabs at her breasts again. She pushes his arm away and refuses to proceed with the washing. (From: M. Borghstijn and W. Johannes, 1992)

Much more threatening for the nurse's general wellbeing are the situations in which the patient or client is physically able and strong. In this context, we should consider not only the patients with mental disorders or a mental handicap, but also those clients not entirely responsible for their own actions. Such as the patients in Kirsten's story, who went far beyond acceptable limits.

No less dramatic are the cases of sexual harassment coming from a completely different direction, namely the (male or female) colleague, the manager or the doctor who seriously breaches the codes of acceptable behaviour by encroaching, uninvited, on what for the nurse is intimate and personal territory.

Nursing Times using a questionnaire, investigated (late 1992) how many of its readers had ever personally had to deal with sexual harassment in the course of their work (McMillan 1993a). An enormous number of the readers responded and completed the questionnaire, and the findings are staggering, particularly with regard to the part played by doctors, superiors, supervisors and colleagues. Nurses, it seems, are even more likely to be harassed by this group than by patients/clients or their relatives (see Table 1.1). We cannot escape the conclusion that nurses have most to fear from the people in their immediate working environment and who, for whatever reason (power, age, experience, reputation or status), feel themselves to be above them.

Many nurses who participated in the *Nursing Times* study explained what had happened to them in detailed written accounts of the incidents. A staff nurse described how as an 18-year-old student nurse she had twice been harassed by two qualified male nurses working on the same ward (McMillan 1993b).

For several weeks, one of them had embarrassed her by extracting sexual connotations from her innocent remarks. This behaviour culminated in his cornering her in the ward's laundry room in an incident which she believes could easily have ended in rape.

'He forced me on to the linen sheets/bags and started to force my legs apart. I managed to struggle enough to bring my knee up and hit him in the groin and quickly unlock the door. I warned him if he tried to do it again I would inform his wife. A few years later I heard that he had been suspended for doing the same thing to another student nurse.'

Table 1.2 – Sexual harassment survey results
(*Nursing Times*, February 24, Volume 89, no. 9, 1993)

**Have you ever been sexually harassed at work or in a
work-related context?**   **97% yes   3% no.**

**What was your most recent experience of being sexually
harassed in a work-related context?**

38%   Hearing sexually suggestive 'jokes' or receiving unwanted
      requests to take part in sexual relationships

25%   Being touched inappropriately on the bottom or breasts

21%   Being touched inappropriately on the back, arms or legs

7%   Being touched on the genitals

4%   Being kissed or touched inappropriately on the face

2%   Being subjected to sexually suggestive looks or comments

2%   Hearing suggestive comments or seeing pictures of naked
      people

1%   Taking part in unwanted sexual intercourse

Where did the sexual harassment take place?

72%   Hospital wards/other units

23%   Non-clinical settings

7%   Own home

8%   Educational setting

7%   Patient's home

10%   Community or social setting

Who sexually harassed you?

30%   Patient or client

3%   Relative of patient or client

17%   Doctor

13%   Immediate supervisor

10%   Senior manager

14%   Other professional

12%   Colleague on same grade

1%   Member of the public

11%   Other

Table 1.2: Sexual harassment survey results
(*Nursing Times*, February 24, Volume 89, no. 9, 1993) (continued)

What type of sexual harassment have you experienced?

63%   Hearing comments about men's or women's appearances

62%   Hearing comments about men's or women's bodies

70%   Member of the opposite sex making comments about your appearance

61%   Sexually suggestive looks

69%   Sexually suggestive jokes

67%   Sexually suggestive teasing

64%   Sexually suggestive questions

49%   Unwanted requests for sexual relationships

25%   Seeing pictures of naked women displayed at work

24%   Seeing pictures of naked men displayed at work

59%   Backs or shoulders being touched inappropriately

55%   Arms or legs being touched inappropriately

50%   Bottom touched

35%   Breasts touched

33%   Face touched inappropriately

Would you welcome training sessions on dealing with harassment?

92%   Yes

Respondents' ages:

18–21   8%

22–29   44%

30–40   30%

41–50   16%

Over 50   2%

Percentages in the tables and in the article have been rounded up or down. Some of the totals do not add up to 100 per cent as the categories listed were not mutually exclusive.

"In another incident, she returned to the same ward on night duty. The night charge nurse asked her to kiss him and hold his hand, which she did. Perhaps in retrospect, she felt flattered. He began touching her, asked her to join him on his ward rounds and offered her lifts home which always ended in a 'detour'.

'I started to cotton on to this and to get scared. So I avoided him and phoned in sick quite a lot until I left this ward', she said. 'Nowadays I would not hesitate to seek help. These two incidents were caused because of my naivety. I feel very embarrassed and extremely angry that I had been so stupid as to let this happen.'" (*Nursing Times*, Feb. 24, vol. 89, no. 8, 1993)

The list of possible traumatic events in which nurses may become involved is thus far from complete. We have, for instance, not yet talked about (attempted) sexual violence against nurses. If the perpetrator has also entered the building unlawfully, the fear of a repetition will have a very decisive effect on the person's life for a long time afterwards. Neither have we looked at the question of collaboration in cases of active or passive euthanasia, which can be extremely upsetting for nurses, or the unbearable suffering of patients whilst the family, doctors or colleagues refuse to bring it to an end – despite knowing full well that the patient would prefer nothing more and has emphatically requested it.

Table 1.3: Possible causes of psychotraumas

- Physical aggression – in psychiatry especially – such as kicking and hitting, particularly if it results in serious physical injury or if the aggression was potentially fatal
- Almost-violent incidents
- (Suspected) contamination or near-contamination with HIV or hepatitis B virus
- Road accidents causing death or serious physical injury (particularly when children are involved)
- Suicide
- Victim of sexual harassment

o Spectator of the death or severe physical injury of a colleague

o Sudden confrontation with death

o Multi-casualty accident

o Having to give nursing care, whilst it is obvious that the patient
  is suffering greatly and there is no hope of recovery or
  improvement

o Serious nursing error, regardless of whether the consequences
  are fatal or serious

o Several small but disturbing incidents within a short period of
  time.

This list is not complete, although it does give an indication of the many
causes of psychotraumas and it does, in any case, illustrate very clearly that
psychological, physical and emotional boundaries (whether or not they
are justifiable and whether or not they are only temporary) have been
exceeded.

The truth is that it is practically impossible to compile a complete
list of traumatizing events. There is always a subjective element in
the impact a particular incident may have on a particular person.
What for one has little or no impact, may cause serious problems
for another. Nor must we overlook the cumulative effect of a series
of 'small' events. And this explains why an apparently insignificant
and ordinary event can throw a nurse of many years' experience
completely off balance.

Here is the story of a nurse working in a hospital emergency
unit:

'Whenever a child is brought here in a serious condition, my
heart skips a beat. A few years ago it almost became too much
for me when I was confronted with three seriously ill children
within a month. First, a child was brought in who had been
having convulsions for nearly an hour; ten days later it was a
child who had been given cytostatics and was having severe
breathing problems on admission; and two weeks later a child,
the son of someone I knew, was admitted with meningitis and
died. During the subsequent period when I went onto night
duty, my knees would start shaking whenever my bleeper went

off: 'as long as it's not a child' was the only thought that went
through my mind.'

It is not the experienced nurses who run the greatest risk of
psychological upheaval, but the newcomers, the relatively young
nurses in particularly. We must not forget that most nurses get their
first hospital experience before the age of 20. And this is an age
group which is focused on gaining a degree of self-confidence,
entering lasting relationships, in search of an individual identity,
and faced in their work with questions such as 'what is the purpose
of life?' or 'why do good people die and bad people live?' And
coping well with the confusing emotions of love is difficult indeed.
But how more difficult is it to handle emotions surrounding
permanent separation, death?

'As a psychiatric nurse, I have seen many young people leave
the profession. Hardly started, and then one suicide after
another. And the repeated aggression. One cannot remain
unmoved by all this.'

A nurse working on an emergency unit writes:

'When you enter the profession, it all makes a very deep
impression on you. I remember a heavily pregnant women
being brought in – a traffic casualty. She was carrying twins,
and she died. We tried to save the children – and two perfect
babies were delivered – a girl and a boy. Lovely black hair, both
dead. This incident did not leave me with a trauma, but the
memory of it will remain with me forever.'

Finally, and ironically, it is precisely the *best* nurses who are most
at risk of being wounded psychologically. An enthusiastic, sympathetic and committed nurse with high ideals is more likely to
become a candidate for a psychotrauma than her less committed
colleague. This explains why the incidence of 'fall-out' as a result
of unresolved traumas is highest among student and newly qualified nurses. Fifteen per cent of nurses under the age of 30 years
suffer 'burn out' within a few years and are on sick leave and/or
join the ranks of those receiving disablement insurance benefits
(Buijssen 1995). An important and preventable cause of this kind

of personal crisis is a psychotrauma which has not been properly worked through.

Definition of a confusing term

There are about as many definitions of the concept of a traumatic event as there are trauma experts. A simple, but very broad, definition is 'any event which causes an unusually intense reaction in an individual'. The definition most widely applied, however – and the one I prefer – is:

> **...an event which lies outside normal human experience and which would cause considerable suffering for almost everyone.**

In other words, it is an event which is so terrible, and so different, that the person concerned can barely cope with it emotionally; i.e. that person has been emotionally wounded by it (the Greek word *trauma* means *wound*).

The term 'trauma' may be confusing to nurses, because for them trauma stands for (serious) physical injury. And there is a second reason for the confusion; as in the case of the word 'stress', the term 'trauma' is used in different ways, first as something occurring outside the person (the event itself), and second as the psychic response to it. 'It was a trauma for him' (compare with: 'He suffers a great deal of stress in his work'), and 'He has been traumatized' ('He is completely stressed').

In order to avoid misunderstandings, we will use the term *shock event* or *incident* when discussing the event itself, and will reserve the term psychotrauma for the human response to it.

What constitutes a shock (or trauma), differs from person to person. One might regard this statement as somewhat contradictory since we have already talked about events 'which would cause considerable suffering for almost everyone', but the contradiction disappears when we concentrate on the *degree of suffering caused by a shock event*. For one person the suffering will be minimal, and for another so great that it disrupts the psychic balance for a considerable period of time. One nurse will have largely forgotten her error (within a week of its occurrence) which accelerated the death of a terminal dementing patient, whilst another nurse committing the same error will find herself in severe psychological crisis months later and apply for sick leave.

The majority of nurses involved in shock events are usually spared the pain of a psychotrauma, and those who are burdened by such a trauma express it in different ways. One will become quiet and withdrawn, another will become cynical, morose and aggressive, a third will seek solace in some kind of addiction (smoking, eating, drinking, buying, sex), and a fourth will develop all kinds of physical disorders (see Tables 1.3 and 1.4).

Table 1.4: Normal physical reactions following disturbing incidents

---

- Tiredness
- Insomnia
- Nightmares
- Breathing problems (e.g. hyperventilation)
- Diarrhoea
- Muscle tension which causes discomfort, such as headache, pain in the shoulder, neck and back
- Irregular menstruation
- Decreased libido
- Confusion, including concentration and memory problems
- Palpitations
- Tremors
- Lump in the throat
- Nausea
- Stomach and intestinal disorders

In many cases, a trauma manifests itself via a cocktail of such symptoms, and in most instances the psychotraumatic reactions diminish in the course of a few weeks. When this fails to happen, however, and the more serious emotional reactions last for at least a month, we are then faced with what is called a post-traumatic stress syndrome (PTSS). A psychotrauma and PTSS share the same symptoms – the primary difference between them is the duration of the symptoms.

The three main features of the psychotrauma (and the PTSS) are:

o re-experiencing reactions (the repeated and 'real' re-experience of the event)

o denial (not feeling, or not wanting to feel, the appropriate emotions) and avoidance of, particularly treat-related situations

o inappropriate arousal ('startle' response).

The first two features might seem again to contradict one another; after all, how can there be re-experiencing reactions on the one hand, and denial on the other hand? The answer to this question penetrates the core of what we know as psychotrauma. The individual involved experiences the two core symptoms not simultaneously but alternately. The traumatized person swings continually between the one extreme of re-experiencing the event in its entirety, and the other extreme of total denial. Experts believe that this being trapped between overwhelming emotions on the one hand, and the absence of emotional expression on the other hand, is the most striking feature of a psychotrauma.

Types of expression

Each of the three main features of a psychotrauma – re-experiencing reactions, denial and heightened inappropriate arousal – can manifest themselves in various ways. In order to be able to recognize a psychotrauma correctly, it is necessary to ponder for a moment on what constitutes its main elements and on the way it manifests itself.

Re-experiencing reactions are in many cases expressed in repeated recall of the event; the nurse sees images of it time and again. Fighting against it does not help. In many cases, the memories are accompanied by unpleasant feelings, such as fear, sorrow, helplessness, aggression and guilt. The images and the emotions combine

Table 1.5 – Normal psychological reactions
following disturbing incidents

Numbing

- because one cannot/does not want to feel/re-live what happened.

Fear

- of collapsing, losing control of oneself, going mad
- of a similar event reoccurring
- of injury or damage to oneself or loved-ones
- of being left alone, losing a loved-one
- of not being able to continue in one's profession
- of other people's reactions
- of not being able to cope with life.

Sorrow

- because of the dead, the wounded and the maimed
- at the loss of one's sense of safety and certainty
- at the loss of one's basic faith in oneself and others
- because one is no longer able to enjoy the normal things of life; there is only apathy.

Feeling of loss

- for what one has lost.

Guilt

- about not having managed better than others; at still being alive or uninjured
- about not having done certain things

Shame

- because of (not) having shown one's emotions, such as sorrow and helplessness
- because of not having reacted as one would have liked
- because of the emotions (such as anger and jealousy) which one has felt in oneself, and which others find unacceptable, or which one feels are inappropriate.

Table 1.5 – Normal psychological reactions
following disturbing incidents (continued)

Anger

- because of what has happened, at the person(s) who caused it, or at allowing it to happen
- because of the shame and humiliation or affront
- because of other people's lack of understanding
- 'Why me?'
- because one has not been properly treated or informed
- towards others who have done so little, made errors or have failed in some way or other.

Powerlessness

- because of anger at the fact that someone else has made a gross intrusion into one's life and because one doesn't know how to handle this anger.

Memories

- of other incidents or losses, such as a loved-one who has died or is handicapped

Jealousy

- towards others who have more happiness.

Alienation

- because one is experiencing emotions not experienced before.

Loneliness

- because one feels different from others who have not experienced the incident or who have experienced it differently
- because the world is still turning round as usual, others are enjoying themselves and making jokes
- because other people do not always respond with understanding.

Despair

- because of the injustice and pointlessness of everything
- disappointments, alternating with:

Hope

- of better times to come.

to give the nurse the impression that she is actually re-experiencing the event itself, i.e. she relives it. The incident can also be relived at night, during sleep – and this means that the nurse suffers terrible nightmares and wakes exhausted and bathed in sweat.

Another type of re-experiencing is that of the person concerned becoming totally out of balance in situations similar to the one in question. If the nurse sees images in a television programme which are reminiscent of those she has experienced herself, the disturbing reactions such as fear, will rise to the surface again.

The second main feature of a psychotrauma is *denial*. The nurse knows that she regularly makes great efforts not to let her thoughts dwell on the incident. She does not want to talk about it and avoids all situations and activities which might remind her of it. The images and the memories are so painful, however, that she invests enormous effort in avoiding anything that will make her think of the event, and it is for this reason that some nurses reach a stage at which they feel compelled to take sick leave. Others turn to drink or smoking to numb their minds, whilst others, for the same reasons, throw themselves into all kinds of activities and hobbies.

Attempts to forget the past, can sometimes be helped by the memory itself; with all the will in the world, a traumatized nurse can no longer recall the important moments of the event.

Memory suppression and avoidance require a great deal of mental energy, and this explains why some nurses are hardly able to summon any interest in the hobbies or activities they used to enjoy. They seem to have no access to the former reality. It is just as if a glass wall has been erected between their present and their past worlds. The world has become a stranger to them and they feel alienated from their own emotions. The nurse is out of contact with her normal feelings, and happiness, joy, anger and hope are shrouded in a dark cloud. She only experiences the 'shadow' of her feelings, and the consequence of this emotional numbing is that she feels there is no future in which she can invest. The horizon has suddenly loomed large in front of her, offering her no perspective, no potential, and life doesn't seem worth living any more.

The third feature of a psychotrauma is *inappropriate arousal,* and this too manifests itself in different ways. A constant and heightened state of alertness is inherent to the nursing profession as a whole – the traffic lights of nursing are never green, but always yellow and it only needs the slightest touch to change them to red at a moment's notice. A nurse in the throes of a psychotrauma can now receive a tremendous shock from an event which would hardly have evoked a raised eyebrow in the past – she has become a frightened rabbit. Being on constant alert for terrible events demands so much of her attention that she finds it very difficult to concentrate on the ordinary, normal activities of her life. She is easily distracted and far more inclined to make mistakes. The heightened irritability is reflected in her general mood – it only takes something very small to throw her completely out of gear in an eruption of anger.

The state of heightened alertness remains even in periods of rest for people suffering from a psychotrauma. The constant worry and brooding have turned sleep into an occasion of tension rather than relaxation.

Nurses with psychotraumas do not usually show all the symptoms mentioned here – the differences between individuals is great. For one, the prime factors will be denial (excessive drinking, for instance), apathy and alienation, and for another it will be aggression and extreme nervousness.

The key word in recognizing a psychotrauma in oneself or someone else, is *different.* One is not what one used to be. A stone has been thrown into the still waters of our own psyche and set it in turmoil.

Risk factors

Some nurses are more prone to developing psychotraumas than others. The most important risk factors are given in the following table:

Table 1.6 – Factors in psychotrauma.

Vulnerability-causing factors

o long and intense confrontation
o vulnerable nature or psychic problems
o family history of psychiatric problems
o limited degree of expectation of the shock event
o limited degree of controllability during the event
o strong identification with the victim
o (imagined) guilt in respect of the event.

Protective factors

o relative degree of expectation of the shock event
o relative degree of controllability of the shock event
o adaptive coping style
o social support.

The first risk factor speaks for itself: the longer and more intensely someone is subjected to a shock event, the higher the risks of after-effects. For many psychiatric patients, for instance, the effects of serious physical abuse often leave more serious psychological scars than a single slap causing no physical injury.

A second vulnerability factor is the individual's own personality. Nurses who by nature are vulnerable as a result of a combination of genetic, psychic and social factors, will more easily lose their psychic equilibrium than nurses of a more stable disposition. Nurses who have been sexually abused in the past (and have never come to terms with it), those needing an above-normal degree of security and clarity, those who are anxious by nature, introvert and reticent types prone to suppressing their feelings – will all find themselves in greater difficulty in the face of a serious situation than their more phlegmatic colleagues.

The same is true of nurses whose powers of adaptability, for other reasons, had already been sorely tested around the time of the incident; divorce or separation, for instance the recent death of a parent, or a miscarriage close to the event. Nurses with a psychiatric history also belong to this risk group.

The third vulnerability factor lies in the family history. The risk of psychotrauma is far greater in nurses from families with a higher than normal incidence of psychiatric disorders (depression, psychosis, for instance). It is within the family that we learn how to cope with problems and calamities. The adaptability style which a child acquires from its parents will often be applied in later life, even if it is not a particularly healthy or effective style.

Another equally important vulnerability factor is the incident's degree of unpredictability. A event that occurs so unexpectedly that the nurse is totally unable to prepare herself for it creates a deeper wound than a foreseeable event. The ambulance nurse sent out to a car accident in which two children are terribly injured will, to a certain extent, be able to prepare herself for the confrontation if, by means of radio contact, she is informed in advance of what she is likely to find on arrival at the scene. The chance that she will experience serious or lasting after-effects is smaller than when she is unexpectedly confronted by the same type of accident.

The fifth vulnerability factor is the limited controllability element, i.e. not being able to intervene or act in the incident. Following the worst traffic accident ever known in the Netherlands in November 1990, which killed eight people and injured another twenty-six, the policemen were psychologically in a worse state than the firemen and ambulance staff. All had seen the same terrible images of carnage on the roads before, but because the police were the first on the scene they could do nothing but watch helplessly as people suffered and died.

The sixth vulnerability factor is the strong sense of identification with the victim. Nurses are usually more deeply moved by suffering and death when it concerns people of their own age, especially if they come from more or less similar backgrounds. This kind of situation inevitably forces the nurse to confront her own vulnerability and mortality. Perhaps even more important than the suffering and death of her contemporaries is the threat to her mental health inherent in the death and suffering of children, especially children of the same age as her own. The ambulance nurse referred to above represented this aspect very forcefully.

The last of the vulnerability factors is the feeling of bearing a degree of guilt for what has happened. It does not matter here whether the guilt is actual and real; all that matters is the experience of it. The nurse who – according to others, against her better judgement – believes that she could and should have prevented the death of a particular patient, finds herself in a far more difficult situation than the nurse who is convinced (rightly or wrongly) that she is blameless. **In short, the manner in which the nurse interprets her own part in it is much more important than the objective aspects of the event.**

Protective factors

There are protective factors, in addition to the vulnerability factors, and the most important are: predictability, controllability, coping style and social support. In the light of what has been stated above, the first two factors require no further explanation, and we will therefore concentrate on the last two.

The term *coping style* points to someone's natural manner of reacting to difficult situations. Broadly speaking, there are two main styles: an active and a passive style. Those who resort to the active style, will react primarily in **doing**, both during and after the emergency situation. They will try to gain control of the situation, go in frantic search of solutions, face up to the confrontation with the surroundings, with others and with themselves. The passive coping style, on the other hand, produces reactions of a more emotional kind, such as turning to drink, taking a holiday, or complaining – come what may, all energy will be diverted to avoiding the confrontation. (Researchers have seen the same type of reaction styles among pigs. If a group of pigs are tied down to the ground on their backs, half of them will put up a long and hard fight to free themselves from the disagreeable situation, whilst the other half will quickly give up the struggle and, literally and figuratively, surrender themselves to their lot.)

Research has shown that people with an active coping style have a greater chance of coming mentally unscathed through a shock event than people with a more passive style. It should be added at this point that the passive coping style is not necessarily, and in all cases, bad or worse than the active coping style; in fact, when there is no possibility of changing the situation or its consequences, a more emotionally passive reaction is often better than the stubborn resistance-against-all-odds approach. Taking a wide berth in the period immediately following an incident can even be a useful strategy to apply; it prevents our taking more mental baggage on board than we can realistically handle. The most effective coping style in the long-term, therefore, is probably a subtle mixture of these two styles.

The most important buffer against stress and the development of psychic disorders, is social support. That means having at least one person who cares, who acts as a sound-board, who stands by us emotionally and makes no judgements on how we are reacting. Those living alone, or in a non-communicative relationship, and who have no one with whom they can share their feelings, are obvious candidates for the psychotrauma risk group.

Why is social support so important? In order to answer this question, we must first talk about that happens when someone becomes a psychotrauma victim. The writer Philip Roth (1993), quoted earlier, presents a perfect picture of what a psychotrauma does to its victim:

'You know what is at the heart of the misery of a breakdown? Me-itis. Microcosmosis. Drowning in the tiny tub of yourself.'

That tub is so small because one's sense of time in the aftermath of a shock incident shrinks to the merely here and now; we can no longer remember who we were before the incident, and it makes us very insecure. Someone sympathetic and close at hand will remind us of who we were – he or she ensures that the link between the I-then and the I-now remains intact, and it puts a firm brake on total despair. A psychotrauma places us, or so it seems, outside our familiar world – just as when someone is told that he is suffering from a serious chronic illness (cancer, for instance). We feel that we no longer belong – we are separated from others and feel alienated from them. Constant support from others brings us, step by step, back to the world we thought we had been evicted from, and the feeling that we are back where we belong brings with it a real sense of healing.

Secondary victimization

Many people do not receive sufficient support because their conception of accepting help from others is incorrect. Some refuse support because they believe it is dangerous to allow anyone else to come too close to them; they say to themselves 'they always want something from you' or 'they will only disappoint or hurt you', and others will say 'only worthless people are interested in me'. These people cannot see help for what it is, because they themselves lack the necessary degree of self-esteem. An even more common attitude is 'other people can never understand how I feel' and refuse support on the grounds that if it isn't 100 per cent, then it's not worth having, or even more frequently because they are afraid of exposing their emotions to others. One of the most important reasons why many nurses do not receive the necessary support is that in the context of coping with disturbing incidents they tend to want to conform to the prevailing culture on their ward. If this is a culture of keeping silent – which is often the case – then most nurses will not have the courage to behave differently from what is expected of them.

A nurse working in an intensive care unit:

'I have been greatly influenced by events involving small children. I had just joined the unit as a student nurse, and had to carry out the doctor's instructions. An hour later the child was dead. And I felt dreadful about it. But I did not talk about it. Because if I had said how awful I had found it, they might have arranged for my dismissal on the grounds that I was not suitable to be a nurse. No one talked about unnerving experiences. In the recreation room a few metres from the intensive care, you hear a lot of cynical remarks. Patients' relatives would be very surprised by it. But it is a means of survival.'

Whatever the reasons may be, barring people from the social support they need (whether or not they choose it) carries a significant risk of their having to shoulder the added burden of a long-term psychotrauma.

For nurses receiving the wrong type of social support, the weight can be even greater. The wrong type of support might, for instance, be a colleague or friend making an inappropriate remark or joke after the incident. A psychiatric nurse, for example, extremely upset by a third suicide in eighteen months on her ward, was not helped by a colleague saying: 'The patients on our ward seem to be dropping down like nine-pins, don't they Nel?' Humour is certainly one way, and sometimes a very effective way, of making a difficult situation bearable, but what is or is not amusing is very much a matter of personal taste. Jokes, therefore, should be used sparingly and with the greatest possible care.

Even worse than 'cheap' attempts to show sympathy, are recriminations, accusations or any other kinds of insensitive reactions from the people around us: 'How could you have been so stupid' or 'You will be in trouble, I'll see to that'. These kinds of remarks only serve to rub salt into the wound, and in the profession are referred to as *secondary victimization* (i.e. creating a double-victim).

Finally, social support stands for nothing if it only involves wanting to hear all the gory details of an incident, more out of a desire for sensationalism than to show empathy.

No social support

What many nurses find in these situations is not so much that they are given the wrong kind of social support, but that they are given *little or no* social support. The people around them refuse to broach the subject of the incident itself and its aftermath or – even worse – are conspicuous by their absence after it.

For the person directly concerned, this is an extremely disappointing experience, and it often pushes her even further into the dark hole of depression. One nurse put it like this: 'If it is true that we really get to know our friends in times of need, then I have very few friends left.' The nurse wonders why others do not *see* that it is precisely at this time that she needs support and understanding, or is it that they don't *want* to see it? Understanding is the first step towards forgiveness, and is therefore extremely important.

In many cases, there is not one, but many reasons why people apparently fail to give the support required. The following list of the most frequent reasons why the necessary support from the immediate environment fails to materialize may throw some light on the problem:

1. The confrontation with another person's misery and sorrow leads to the realization of one's own vulnerability and mortality ('The same thing could happen to me, but I would rather not think about it').

2. Most of us have never learned how to approach sorrow and setbacks in a sensible way ('My parents always said "don't whine"').

3. We often don't feel we are the right person to offer help ('I'm not close enough to her').

4. Fear of being overcome by one's own emotions ('If she starts to tell me exactly what happened, I'll start to cry too').

5. People feel themselves to be helpless and powerless ('I don't know what I should do to help her').

6. Fear that bringing up the subject again will only make matters worse and increase the pain ('Who knows what will come flooding out').

7. Fear that giving help will cost a great deal of time and energy ('If I begin to help her, she will never let me go').

Recognizing a psychotrauma

The psychotrauma has only recently begun to attract interest. Were people immune to psychotraumas in the past? Why is it that the psychological consequences of dramatic incidents were never talked about before?

It is highly probable that psychotrauma has existed throughout the history of mankind. The clearest evidence of this is that the features of a psychotrauma experienced by our distant ancestors, the primates, become apparent when they too are confronted by disturbing events. Baby apes react traumatically when they become separated from their mothers. After a few days of crying and protest, they simply give up and sink into apathy and depression. And if they are later reunited with their mothers, they are incapable of a pleasurable reaction to it. They have been psychologically wounded, and they carry traces of it for the rest of their lives; they remain psychologically more vulnerable than other apes.

It was only at the end of the last century that psychologists and psychiatrists began to study the consequences of disturbing events in humans. The French psychiatrists, Charcot and Janet, and the world's best known psychiatrist who followed in their footsteps, Sigmund Freud, were the first to treat patients suffering from symptoms which could be related back to some earlier disturbing event.

They were concerned with women suffering from hysteria – initially a liberating diagnostic label, it later became a very 'loaded' term indeed. The term 'hysteria' stood for physical disorders arising from events which were so intensely disturbing that they were banished from the memory. And because the mind never surrenders unpunished to pressure, the psychological pain turns into physical pain. Freud initially suggested (at the end of the last century), that hysteria was the result of perverse (traumatizing) acts occurring in a child's early years. When it became apparent that hysteria also occurred among the upper classes of society (Freud's own clientele), and that this viewpoint threatened to isolate him, he turned the theory around and declared that women were fantasizing their perverse stories. After this, fundamental research into the causes of hysteria died an early death. In the revised viewpoint, a disturbing event now became something that had not really happened.

(The world had to wait until the 1980s before research suggested that Freud's original conception was all too true: at least 15 per cent of the women appear to have been the childhood victims of incest or undesired physical intimacies within their own family circles. And it was not until 1994 that a Dutch researcher in studying Freud's letters to his friend Fliess, discovered that the founder of psychoanalysis had, just as his brothers and sister, been sexually abused by his father during his youth. The person who first suggested the suppression mechanism, had thus himself suppressed this incest experience.)

Some 40 per cent of the millions of soldiers serving in the trenches of World War I, developed symptoms very similar to those Freud described in his hysterical women: loss of speech, numbing, loss of memory, uncontrollable crying. They had seen too much misery and terror: eight million soldiers lost their lives in those four exhausting years of the war.

Because it was feared that if the real cause of the massive psychological collapse on the Front were made known it would have a demoralizing effect on both the troops themselves and the home front, the symptoms were initially recorded as being of physical origin: wounding as a result of exploding hand grenades. The official diagnosis was *shell shock*. When it was established that the symptoms also occurred in people with no physical injury, the military psychiatrists had to adjust their diagnosis and admit that the cause of the suffering was psychological. Science obediently toed the line of the military machine and immediately made hasty moves to look for links between the development of a psychotrauma and a person's individual character. 'Real men were psychologically indestructible, only their weaker brothers succumbed.' In popular parlance, the psychologically wounded front line soldiers were labelled deserters and cowards.

After the war ended, interest in psychotraumas began to wane among doctors, psychologists and researchers, but was given new life during World War II; they even discovered a very successful treatment. In broad terms, this was the same as is currently used today: allow patients to talk a great deal about the event, and restore their contacts with their own people, the fighting unit. Once the war was over, interest in psychotraumas faded again.

It was another 30 years before the tide turned; the 1970s saw the return of many thousands of demoralized American troops from the battlefields of Vietnam. They still suffered from terrible nightmares many years after their homecoming, they felt guilty about what they had done and could no longer enjoy the things they had enjoyed so much before. A high percentage had become addicted to drugs. Many divorced because they were no longer capable of participating in a normal relationship.

Because they found no response within the traditional mental health care system for their problems, they organized fellow-sufferer meetings during which they could discuss their war-stories in detail together. Within a few years, many hundreds of these self-help groups had been established. The war veterans began to organize themselves more and more, and in the wake of public opinion steadily changing its judgement of the war from *just* to *pointless*, they were able to gather increasing political power. They were able to obtain funds to finance systematic research into the psychological consequences of war for the demobilized troops. This kind of research proved that there is a direct link between war experiences and the disorders occurring among the Vietnam veterans.

The real recognition followed in 1980; in that year the manual of the American Psychiatric Association included for the first time, the diagnosis *post-traumatic stress disorder*. It was a turning-point and a milestone, because the manual is not only a bible for American psychiatrists and psychologists, but also for professionals involved in mental health care services throughout the world.

It also appeared that the diagnosis had a much larger application-area than war victims alone; the symptoms they suffered were also encountered in victims of incest, maltreatment, shipping disasters, assaults, traffic accidents, rape, in relatives involved in suicide cases and the survivors of the concentration camps. The survivor is regularly confronted with flash-backs which he attempts to suppress, he is jittery and feels isolated.

It was not until the 1990s that the media began to show a wide interest in psychotraumas, and to inform the general public about the symptoms, causes and treatment. One effect of informing the public in this way was that professionals were also compelled to become better informed. Until recently, the average Mental Health Care Centre worker, front-line psychologist, psychiatrist or social worker, had hardly any awareness of the most elementary principles of psychotrauma treatment. Neither were general practitioners equipped to recognize the connection between their patient's symptoms now and their having experienced a deeply disturbing incident in the past.

Health institutions such as hospitals, psychiatric centres, nursing homes and home nursing organizations, only realized fairly recently that nurses and nursing assistants too can become traumatized by situations encountered during their work. And, needless to say, there were hardly any support or treatment provisions. This situation is fortunately changing fast.

Chapter 2

Coming to Terms
A Guideline for Self-Help
and Support

Introduction

This chapter, which is all about coming to terms with a psychotrauma will begin, by way of introduction, with a thought experiment.

Let us just imagine. After having saved for four years you buy a new car, and one day you use it to go shopping. When you come out of the supermarket and walk back to the car park, you find the car has gone.

You cannot believe your eyes. Although you are certain where you left the car, you still make a thorough search of the car park: 'Perhaps I was wrong about where I parked it', or 'has someone else parked it somewhere else?' (a strange thought, but you never know...).

Your search produces nothing, and you decide to report the theft immediately to the police.

And here comes the question to the reader. How many times will you tell this story in retrospect? Will you only tell it to your wife, your girl friend or your mate? Will you tell him or her the story just once or more often? Or will you also tell your parents, your neighbour, your brother, sister and anyone who will listen to it? Will you, however disagreeable the whole event was for you, burden your friends, colleagues and acquaintances with it too? Will you stop telling the story after a week, because by that time you will have been able to put the theft behind you?

Don't forget that we are only talking about a car here – something replaceable. How often will you have to tell a story of an incident that has had a much greater impact on your life; a story about a human life; an incident which rocks the very foundation of both your professional and family life?

How long and how often would you want to talk about an event which had undermined your former confidence and changed your past, your present and your future?

What does 'coming to terms' mean?

The saying 'time heals all wounds' seems to suggest that grief and anguish will heal by themselves in time – but, unfortunately, that is not the case. Coming to terms with a psychotrauma involves enormous effort. It requires, in fact, the same degree of physical and mental effort as top sport. The weight of working-through a psychotrauma comes from the confrontation that has to be faced with the painful emotions we have been discussing so far – particularly in talking things through with others or with oneself. Not just once, but time and time again. By giving in to the feelings we would rather not have to talk about because they are so terribly painful, ultimately puts a kind of padlock on our capacity to speak. We have tried to give a visual impression in Figure 2.1 of how a psychotrauma is worked-through.

These five lines represent the same number of conditions to which our psychic constitution is heir. The upper line represents the rare state of supreme happiness, such as being in love or at the birth of one's child. The dotted line represents the condition of normal happiness, meaning a general state of well-being. The lowest line represents a condition of deep psychic suffering (such as during a period of severe depression), and the dotted line above it brings us into the area of feeling rotten and miserable. The greater part of our lives is played out in the area around the middle line; we generally fluctuate, therefore, between the two dotted lines.

When we are suddenly 'hit' by some kind of shock event, the line of our normal state of mind (shown in Figure 2.1) makes a sharp downward dive. We don't realize this immediately because we are more or less numbed by what has happened – but as the

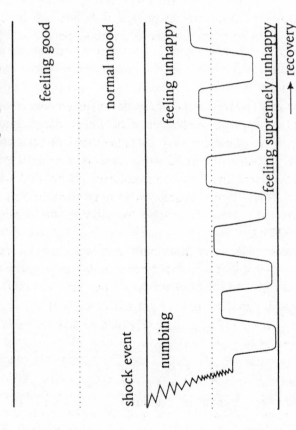

Figure 2.1 A visual representation of how people come to terms with a psychotrauma

numbing effect wears off, we begin to feel extremely unhappy. As we start to think about the shock event, our state of mind falls to an even lower 'low', and because when our pain and misery – so extreme, sometimes, that we can even imagine we are going mad – pulls us down to the level below the upper dotted line, we tend to seek refuge in the upper regions. Because those around us also feel unhappy in the presence of our suffering, they too try instinctively to pull us upwards. This might take the form of changing the subject of conversation or bringing any talk to an abrupt end with the words: 'life must go on'.

In order to recover completely from a psychic shock, we have no choice but to accept the confrontation with the feelings within the two lines of emotion presented in our diagram above. And that is an extremely painful exercise, although it should be remembered that the pain diminishes with each successive confrontation; we take thereby a small step upwards out of our dark hole and, slowly but surely, we come closer to the mood-area we were in before the event.

Marcel Proust, not only one of the greatest writers of this century but also one of the world's giants in understanding the intricacies of the human mind, once wrote: 'We only recover from mental pain by suffering it completely'. And to put it another way: we must not go *around* it but *through* it, or as the American pop-singer Melissa Ethridge once said:

'My father died last year. He had liver cancer. That was painful, very painful. But I knew that if I allowed myself to feel the grief, I would not be confronted by it later; that I would not, ten years later, still have to come to terms with my father's death. It would allow me later to be just as happy then as I was sorrowful at that moment. Happier even, I am sure of that.'

The same is true of coming to terms with a traumatic event. No one can escape the coming to terms, unpunished and without pain. If we do try to do that, however, we will have to pay the price via the emergency exits and back roads of our minds and bodies, and in all kinds of disguises; perhaps in the shape of a disturbing lump in the throat, eczema or hyperventilation attacks. Unworked-through traumatic events have put many nurses on long-term sick-leave, and for some it has meant sickness benefits and the end of a career.

The psychotrauma goes about its destructive work like a smouldering moorland fire deep underground. The longer we wait, the more difficult it is to put the fire out. People who carry their psychotrauma around in secret are damaging their own health – as so many studies have so clearly proved.

Bergsma (1994) referred to one study in which several hundred students were asked if they had experienced a traumatic event recently or at some time during their youth. Had their parents divorced, for instance; had a brother or sister committed suicide; had they ever been raped or sexually abused, robbed or physically attacked? And they were then asked if they had ever talked of these events with anyone else. It became apparent that students who had tried to come to terms with their traumatic experiences alone, were more often troubled by major and minor illnesses. Students with no psychotraumatic histories, or who had talked about them in detail to others, were generally healthier.

No one can go on for ever trying to cope alone with the after-effects of a shock event. The human mind, which works extremely effectively at moments of severe psychic turmoil, makes sure that this need not happen. What happens then? The confrontation is dosed, as it were, so that the pain is never more than we can actually take. The denial which follows each dose of confrontation is necessary in order to gather our strength and recover our balance in the wake of the pain that preceded it. Coming to terms with a shock event, therefore, is characterized, as we have already said, by the fact that the re-experience and the denial alternate with one another. By allowing ourselves to dive into the pool of misery, on the one hand, and to follow it by stubbornly burying our heads in the sand, we gradually regain our equilibrium and return to who we were before the event.

The first days and weeks following a shock event are usually dominated by re-experiencing and confrontation symptoms; repeated repetition of images, memories and nightmares. This period is followed by a predominantly denial phase; lack of interest, no desire to talk about the incident, emotional numbness.

In summary: to recover fully from an event of great impact on our lives, we must accept the confrontation, although it need not be continuous. If we try to avoid the pain forever, it will ultimately lead to physical or mental disorders of one kind or another. The price to be paid for silence and suppression, is pain of a longer duration. Emotions have no expiry date; if they are not expressed, they will not go away. Sooner or later they will bubble to the surface. There is no recipe for recovery without pain.

Necessary illusions

We might ask ourselves what purpose coming to terms serves ('after all, what has happened has happened' or 'what is done cannot be undone'). Why not simply just go on, rather than look back forever at the past? That is often said when someone continues to talk about an incident that has had absolutely no physical conse-quences, such as physical aggression without injury or a nursing error corrected in the nick of time. No scratches, no broken leg and still injured?

The reason why we cannot simply step over a shock event, is that the incident has affected the certainties and assumptions which are the foundations upon which our psychic well-being rests. We all think we have a great deal of control over our existence, and we all know that every time we step into a car, we run the risk of being involved in an accident. We all possess this knowledge but none of us really thinks we will be the next one on the list of traffic victims – 'that happens to other people, not to me'. In fact, if we really did believe we would be the next car accident victim, we would sit almost paralyzed at the steering wheel. In other words, the illusion of invulnerability does have a purpose – it enables us to do what we have to do, including taking charge behind the steering wheel, relaxed and confident.

The nurse also knows that she is capable of making a fatal error, but if she were to constantly think about the possibility in her daily working life, she would become very tense and make mistakes because of it. The psychiatric nurse knows too, when she travels to her work in the morning, that she could be confronted by a violent patient, but does not to say to herself 'let's hope I arrive home in once piece tonight'. Just as drivers believe that they will not have an accident if they take the necessary care, so too do nurses believe that no serious errors will be made if they do their work well, and that they will not be attacked if they follow the proper procedures.

Another deeply-rooted idea is that our world must be just. We do not believe that someone who works for the good of others will be harmed or punished. For the maternity nurse, therefore, it is totally preposterous that she should be hindered in her work by the completely inappropriate and uninvited behaviour of the infant's father. 'This is not just – surely this is not the way the world is meant to be.' A shock event cruelly disturbs the illusion that we have our destiny in our own hands. Our former certainties suddenly become uncertainties; our lives are shaken to the core, and that steadfast belief that 'it will not happen to me' is shattered for all time.

Coming to terms means that we have to clear the debris of the psychic 'earthquake' and put things back in place. We have to rebuild and create order out of the chaos; we have to regain our faith (in ourselves and in others) so that we can, to a certain extent at least, take control of our lives again.

Why confrontation is necessary

Confronting the incident is absolutely vital, and for various reasons. First, the repeated and painful process of confrontation gives us the opportunity of getting used to the necessary emotional upheaval, so that the incident itself no longer has such an unsettling effect on us. By repeatedly going back to the incident in our minds, the intense emotional pain slowly diminishes. The traumatized person becomes used to the idea of what has happened. When we keep discovering that following a confrontation we are psychically still standing with our feet firmly on the ground, we gradually regain our former strength and confidence. It is like the fear some people have of water: by splashing about, ducking under and coming up again, we slowly lose our fear.

Repeated confrontation helps us to build-up a new image of the world. Only by allowing ourselves to churn the event over in our minds again and again can we adjust and re-define our definitions of justice, certainty, security or trust. The new answers arise from the constant process of thinking the event through, with questions such as 'What actually happened?' and 'Why did it happen?', 'Why me?', 'Am I to blame?' and 'What is the point of it all?'

Finally, the repeated confrontation can also be useful because it helps to prevent a subsequent incident. By the frequent re-running of the 'film' and the search for a cause, exit roads and emergency escape routes, we discover ways of avoiding similar incidents in the future, or of reacting differently and more effectively if something like it should happen again.

Coping strategies

The main aims of the coping process are the search for meaning and the regaining of control, and there are four strategies aimed at achieving these goals (Van den Bout and Kleber 1994):

1. search for an explanation
2. tell the story
3. compare with others
4. positive interpretation.

The search for an explanation

It is a misconception to think that coming to terms is a purely emotional process. During the period immediately following the event, the heart of the matter lies in finding the answers to just two very logical questions: 'what happened?' and 'why?', and after a short interval this is followed by question number 3 'why me?' Some people accuse themselves of reacting too rationally, too calmly, to a drama.

Wanting an explanation and wanting to understand, however, is far from pointless. The search for an explanation is part and parcel of the coping. No one finds rest if they do not know what happened and why; and this explains why people who have made a successful recovery from the after-effects of a personal drama have nearly always managed to find an explanation for what happened. To outsiders, these explanations sometimes lack credibility, but for the people directly concerned an explanation is so very important that they will go to great lengths to find it.

People will keep worrying about it and continue the search until they find something that will explain it. Answers like: 'It might just as easily *not* have happened' or 'it was pure chance' bring no satisfaction, because they leave no room for personal control or personal intervention. Most people, therefore, start the quest for an answer by blaming someone, usually themselves, especially at the beginning 'If only I had…' or 'if only I had not…'. If we put the blame for the incident on ourselves, it means we can avoid a similar event in the future – by taking greater care, by being more sensible, by being more alert. Self-accusation triumphs over that feeling of helplessness; blaming ourselves, therefore, is not so foolish as it might at first seem.

We often see that a victim will at a later stage look beyond himself for the cause of the suffering and place the blame, for instance, at the door of the management responsible for the running of the institution, the doctors, a matron, a colleague. And it is often only in the last phase of coming to terms that someone traumatized by a particular event can get it into its true perspective. He or she discovers, for instance, that people – despite doing their very best – sometimes make mistakes and that some mistakes do have fatal consequences.

Telling the story

The most important strategy for rising above a shock event is to talk about it. The nastiest symptom of a psychotrauma is the repetition-reaction which threatens our sense of being in control: the images of the incident come uninvited and often at inconvenient moments. By telling the story of what happened, we gain control of it.

This happens initially in a rather chaotic manner. A nurse telling her traumatic story for the first time is seldom able to do so with any clear line in it. She will usually jump from one aspect to another, and because it will cost her great effort to keep her emotions under control, she will fall over her own words. She is fully aware of what is happening and offers her excuses for being so difficult to follow, such as: 'Sorry, but I really can't help it — there are so many thoughts racing around in my head at the moment.'

By telling her story time after time, she gradually begins to give it structure and bring order into the chaos of her thoughts. Details and special points of interest which she at first was not able to remember, now slowly slip into their proper place.

There is another reason why reconstructing and structuring her story helps the nurse to regain control of her life; emotions and events which almost 'drowned' her until recently can now be lucidly formulated and made part of a cohesive whole. The more clarity and cohesion we can bring into our story (first this happened, and then that, followed by…etc.), the more control we have over what happened to us and the more we can take the reins of our past firmly in our own hands again. The event which was at first so overwhelming can now be given its rightful place in our lives – it no longer controls us, we control it. This is why allowing someone to tell his or her story in full, and repeatedly, is the best thing any of us can do – whether it be in the light of self-help, support from the people around, or professional help.

'I was trained at the time when you had to behave as if you could take everything. You were expected to find it quite normal when a patient was forcefully transferred to the isolation cell, even though you felt it was awful. My daughter is now doing her training in the same hospital and I often say to her: 'don't give the appearance of being tougher than you are. If you have problems, talk about them.' Fortunately, there is much better support now. She was recently hit rather hard by a patient, but was able to talk about it immediately and say how she felt at

the time. A considerable improvement. If you have difficulties
with something, you do not automatically become a "softy".'

Not everyone is able to talk to others about his or her deepest
feelings, or to expose his or her vulnerability to others; these
people, in fact, are helped by their committing the incident to
paper. It is important, however, that they do not restrict themselves
simply to noting how they feel ('I feel so unhappy and desperate
today'), but that they also try to relate their story in the form of a
written reconstruction.

Just how important this can be became very apparent in an
experiment in which test subjects were asked, during the course
of four successive days, to write an account of a traumatic event in
their lives (Bergsma 1994). It appeared to improve their general
health and the functioning of their immune systems. Other test
subjects were asked during the experiment to confine themselves
to a written account of their emotions during the traumatic event
in question. They were thus limited to writing only about feeling
afraid, confused, angry or helpless, without being able to translate
the psychotrauma into a coherent written story. This too, of course,
produced positive effects, but less than in the other full-story
group.

Comparison with others

Another strategy which psychotrauma victims apply is comparison
with others. In the immediate aftermath of the incident, these
people will usually compare themselves with others who have
apparently done better. They are angry at them, they feel ashamed
and jealous ('why me?').

In the course of time, however, their frames of reference
undergo a shift: instead of looking upwards, they now tend to look
downwards – to people who have had even worse experiences.
They climb up, as it were, on the back of those who have suffered
even more, and thus repolish their sense of personal esteem. Or
they comfort themselves with the thought that it could all have
been much worse: 'fortunately, I only have a few scratches and my

face has not been damaged at all'. Indeed, 'I'm a very lucky devil' is the proud conclusion of one psychiatric nurse.

In order to make these kinds of comparison, contact with fellow-sufferers is essential. By comparing notes, we discover that others in similar situations have also had a very difficult time, and that is a comforting thought.

Positive interpretation

Some people are natural winners, and others are born losers. Psychological research has shown that the difference between *a winner* and *a loser* usually has nothing to do with the degree of fortune or misfortune in a person's life. A contented and happy 70-year-old can have had on average as many setbacks as a younger person who looks back with bitterness on his life. The distinction between the two is that the former has been able to turn his loss into profit, and the latter has not.

Johan Cruijff (of Ajax fame), following his (first) 'retirement' as a professional footballer, lost all his capital after investing in a pig-breeding farm with a dishonest partner. When Cruijff was asked years later how he regarded the experience in retrospect, he said: 'I am glad it happened to me, it has made me stronger and taught me a lot.' This is a comment typical of a natural winner.

People who manage ultimately to rise above a shock event, usually do so in much the same way as Johan Cruijff. They say that it gave them greater insight both into themselves and others, adding that they are able to distinguish between what is important and what is less important, and that they now know what life is all about.

Self-help tips

In this chapter, we have looked at the current theories on the question of coming to terms with a psychotrauma. When someone has been involved in a deeply shattering event, however, he/she often does not have the energy to read and absorb a long theoretical discourse on what you should know and what you should do in such a situation; he/she lacks the capacity to concentrate on, and absorb, the full meaning of a long and detailed text.

For this reason, we present some practical guidelines, in the form of two *check lists*, for people who find themselves in extremely difficult situations and who develop, or are likely to develop, serious psychological after-effects.

The first list contains a number of self-help tips, many of which deal with the theoretical approaches we have already discussed, but which are now translated into concrete and practical approaches. The second list is intended for people who feel they are stuck, as it were, unable to move forward, and it offers guidelines on recognizing the 'signs' which point to the need for professional help.

In my experience, professionals involved in the type of situations we have been talking about are less likely to call in professional help than the non-professionals. It appears, for instance, that in practice many nurses struggle on alone and for far too long with their private internal battles. This is a pity, because we know that the chances of recovery from psychic problems decreases in proportion to their duration.

Check list 1: What can you do yourself?

- Try to get the incident in focus in your mind and acknowledge that it has happened.

- Allow time for the natural, slow but sure process of recovery.

- Give yourself time to relax and enjoy things, and follow your usual routine as much as possible; in other words, alternate confrontation with distraction.

- Do not bottle-up your emotions, express them openly. Let your partner and your children participate in your sorrow.

- Do not avoid talking about what you have experienced. Take every opportunity to talk it through with others. Or do this in your thoughts, alone in your own mind. Allow yourself to be part of a group of people who love you, or with whom you feel 'at home'.

- Show your vulnerability and be willing to accept support. Practical and emotional support from other people can make things much more bearable. Do not reject them. There is much to be gained by sharing your experiences with people in the same sort of situation. Barriers can fall away and relationships become more profound.

- Do not expect the memories to fade (quickly); the accompanying images and emotions will remain with you for a long time.

- Keeping yourself busy, for instance by helping others or by doing light jobs, can lessen the load on your shoulders. Being over-active, however, is not advisable, because it can squeeze out the attention and help you need for yourself.

- Allow yourself (sufficient) time for sleep, for rest, for reflection and for being with friends and family. You too need rest and distraction. And in order to keep your emotions in balance, you will also need to be alone from time to time.

- Be clear and honest towards family, friends and colleagues about your needs. This means telling them what you want and what you need.

- Try, when the initial deeply emotional phase has passed, to lead as normal a life as possible. Staying at home for a long period will not bring you further; on the contrary. Try to continue working, or to resume your work as soon as possible. Try to avoid difficult and pressing situations; work more in the background.

- Surround yourself with living things: people, animals, plants.

- Try to express your emotions in the written word, or in painting, drawing or music.

- Drive more carefully than before, and take care when doing odd (or dangerous) jobs in and around the house.

- Be prepared for the fact that not everyone will show the same degree of understanding and sympathy towards your difficulties or your story.

o Realize that the first all-consuming emotions will diminish in the course of time.

o Realize that one event can release emotions attached to another earlier event (a death in the family, for instance).

o Avoid having to make important decisions and choices, such as moving house, a new job, the ending of a relationship etc. That can all come later.

o If you feel you are not getting enough support, do not hesitate to take the initiative yourself in asking for it. It often happens that others appreciate the trust we place in them.

o Realize that a relationship becomes stronger and more stable in proportion to the degree of balance between giving and taking. However difficult you find it, and however much effort it costs you, therefore, try to talk about things other than yourself. Make a habit of asking how things are with the other.

o Realize that an apparent lack of response does not mean that the people around you are not interested in you and that they do not want to help you. Many people will want to help you but will not know how to approach you. Some will even avoid you on the street because they don't quite know what to do in the circumstances. (Perhaps you have also done this yourself in the past.)

o Do not enter a sort of contest with your fellow sufferers as to who is having most difficulty.

o Realize that forgiveness (yours and others') is an essential part of the healing process.

o Try as far as possible to restore your daily routine to what it was before the shock event: getting up in the morning, meal times, household activities etc.

o Be very careful in using sleeping tablets, anti-depressants and tranquillizers. Use them only occasionally; never for longer than 10–14 days.

○ Re-read these tips often.

Warning: accidents occur more often during periods of severe stress (cause: lower concentration and alertness).

Check list 2: When to call in professional help?

○ When you feel you cannot cope any longer with the intense emotions and physical reactions; when you have the feeling that you cannot place emotions correctly, when you feel chronically tense, confused, empty or exhausted; when you repeatedly feel compelled to take sick leave because your work demands so much of your energy; when physical symptoms (such as headaches, stomach disorders, lack of appetite) do not disappear.

○ When, after a month, you still feel numb and empty and that your feelings are not the same as everyone else's in a similar situation (see above). When you have to keep yourself busy in order not to 'feel' anything.

○ When nightmares (especially about the incident) and sleeplessness persist.

○ When you have, or know, no one with whom you can share your feelings and you feel you need it nonetheless.

○ When you notice that your relationship(s) is/are coming under pressure and have also suffered as a result of the shock event, or if added problems have arisen. Such as rows at work or in your private life.

○ When you have various (smaller) accidents.

○ When you find yourself still smoking and drinking more, some time after the traumatic event.

○ When you notice that someone in your immediate environment (e.g. a colleague) appears to be extra vulnerable or is not making the appropriate recovery.

○ When you become obsessed with the fear of the incident recurring.

o When you react differently, or out of all proportion, to events or persons both within and outside your work situation.

o When you realize some considerable time after the event (a year, for instance), that you are still not functioning as you did prior to the event, and that you also see no ascending line of improvement. When you remain exceptionally irritable.

o When your guilt feelings, fear, hate or feelings of revenge have not lessened after a reasonable period of time.

o When you regularly hear from the people around you that you have changed (e.g.: have become quiet, reticent, easily irritated, negative, complaining, non-joking, only cynical).

o When, after a month, you are still not able to enjoy anything.

o When, within a month, you have had four or more panic attacks.

o Realize that, in essence, you are the same person you were before the disaster or incident happened. Do not forget that there is always light at the end of the tunnel. Realize that if you are suffering too much or too long, professional help is always available.

Tips for family, friends, neighbours, colleagues etc.

In the last chapter, we saw how important it is for the traumatized nurse, for instance, to receive help from those around her. Few indeed succeed through their own efforts in absorbing the full blast of a severe psychic set-back, and the personal stories which opened this book have shown that proper help does not come automatically. None of us has really learned how to approach our own psychic pain, let alone that of another. This means that when we are confronted by someone else's pain and distress, we very often have no idea what we should say or do.

Our clumsiness in facing other people's distress was illustrated in a study carried out by Davidowtz and Myrick in 1984, when they analyzed the kind of statements made by people in the vicinity of those mourning the loss of a loved one. The researchers restricted themselves to the close relatives; people who were obviously very concerned and involved.

'Comforting' remarks were placed on a continuum from helpful to non-helpful. Examples of the first category were remarks such as: 'Tell me how you are feeling', 'How can I help you?', 'Call in on me or give me a ring whenever you feel the need'. Examples of non-helpful comments were: 'I know how you feel', 'Time heals all wounds', 'Life must go on' or 'Try not to think about it all the time'.

To their surprise, the researchers found that 80 per cent of the comments, of those involved, could be categorized as non-helpful, to a lesser or greater degree. The study showed that most people are of little help verbally, and experience has taught me that the same is often also true of social workers, doctors and nurses and so forth, many of them much preferring to avoid subjects such as loss and grief altogether. Professionals, like so many non-professionals, also tend to think that they will make matters worse by talking about them – 'You never know what you are likely to unleash'.

Another common myth is the idea that we increase emotional pain by opening up a conversation about its cause. In short, present-day society is very wary of loss, afraid of emotions and few of us know how to approach our own and other people's pain. This is particularly so of men. It also explains why people caught up in a psychotrauma often fall in, what to them feels like, a black hole and report that they experience no real understanding from those around them.

One must in all honesty add here that the person in that 'black hole' does not always make it easy for his/her family or associates. Many traumatized people are ambivalent in the face of assistance from outside. A mixture of pride, shame and alienation often block the simple acceptance of help, whilst deep inside these same people are actually screaming out for support. The person directly concerned in this inner conflict is often not fully in control of himself and sometimes he does things he later regrets.

I came across a very good example of this in the novel *Scarred Tissue* by Michael Ignatieff (1994). The main character of the book describes openly how he behaved towards his loved ones, particularly his wife and children, following the death of his father.

'I admit I must have been impossible to live with. It was the self-righteousness of the grieving – my idea that I would betray him if I carried on as before, if I went through the motions of living – that must have driven my family apart from me. I still do not understand those instincts that lead you to flee the ones who want to help you, that lead you to take revenge upon them for a sorrow that is not their fault. I look back over this period and scarcely understand anything I did. I felt in the grip of some fatality, when in fact I could have stopped myself at any moment. After a life of apparent sanity and control, I discovered reservoirs of gratuitous destructiveness I had never imagined I possessed. Looking back now, I seem to have been entranced by it, enraptured by my capacity to do harm.'

Because so many of us do not know how to offer help, the following check list presents a number of practical ideas on how to be supportive of traumatized relatives, friends or colleagues.

Section 3.7 of the following chapter, contains more practical ideas.

Check list 3 – Tips for helping others

- Maintain contact, remain available, even when the other person's response is unwilling and rejecting. Visit him/her regularly and invite him/her to your home.

- Do not talk immediately of the future, but focus more on the present and the past.

- Try to remain, in your response to him/her, as true to your own feelings as possible.

- Allow the other person to cry. Crying takes the steam off the emotional kettle. It is healing.

- Touch the other person. People who have endured a deeply intrusive event in their lives, often experience a physical emptiness. They often feel the need for a comforting arm around their shoulders or an embrace. When words fail, a touch can do wonders.

○ Do not say too much yourself initially. Let the other person do the talking. Ask questions such as 'what happened exactly?', 'who was there?', 'how did your colleagues, superior, partner, react?, especially.

○ Repeat, briefly, what you think you understand the other person to be saying: 'I imagine that you simply thought you were administering the same medicine as you always did.' 'If I understand you correctly, you are now accusing yourself of not picking up the signals which would have indicated an impending suicide.'

○ Realize that the person concerned is often very afraid in the early phase, and that he/she longs for company. It is usually more important at this stage simply to 'be there' in the background, than to talk at length.

○ Be very cautious about making jokes about the situation, however well-meaning you may be.

○ Do not try to precipitate the recovery process – let it take its course.

○ Do not condemn the person's aggressive and guilt feelings.

○ Treat the person concerned as a normal human being; do not be over-serious or particularly worried. And do not be unnaturally jolly.

○ Do not tell someone how he/she should feel ('you must be feeling pretty hopeless now').

○ If you want to give comfort and help but do not know how, you could say something like: 'I am truly concerned about you and would love to be able to say something to comfort you, but I don't know what.'

○ Do not use the person's story to lead into a similar story about yourself or a colleague, for instance. The person's own story is the point of focus. If you really cannot avoid relating a similar story, keep it very short and return immediately to the other.

o Do something concrete for the other person. Write a card or a letter, send or bring flowers. Do not be over-critical: better something than nothing. The most important thing is that the other knows you have him/her in your mind.

o Do not be impatient, and realize that someone who has experienced a shock event often needs to tell the same story time and time again.

o Try to involve the other in activities you used to do together, such as tennis, cycling, walking, jogging, volley ball etc. If you notice that the other is hesitant or evasive, give him/her a gentle 'push'.

o Do not give (cheap) advice like 'try to sleep', 'take a short holiday or go somewhere for the day', 'try to look a bit happier'. No one needs this type of advice. If the other person wants advice, he/she will ask for it.

o Avoid cliches same as: 'you are not the only one to whom this kind of thing has happened', 'put it behind you', 'talking about it will not undo it', or 'that is a professional hazard, it's all part of the job'.

o Examples of more helpful reactions are: 'tell me how you really feel', 'have a good cry', 'you are very strong'.

o Re-read these tips more than once.

Chapter 3

Support Within an Institution

Introduction

A psychiatric nurse:

'The institution where I worked was located right next to the railway line. One evening, a train was standing still on the track closest to the institution – an unusual place for it to be. When I went to have a look, the train-driver told me that a body was lying on the track in front of the train. One of our own patients had thrown himself under the wheels of the speeding train – he had been decapitated. I told the train-driver that I would inform the institution and would return. The driver replied that he had warned the railway police, and having said this he made a hasty retreat. And there I was: more or less alone in the darkness.

The police arrived after a while. Out of a sort self-protection mechanism, I announced that I was a professional nurse, but that I had no experience with corpses on the railway line. The police were reasonably good in their support, and some time later a number of my colleagues finally appeared on the scene. When I asked why it had taken them so long (20 minutes), they replied "Oh, we knew you were here", as if that made any difference.

The following day – I was not feeling exactly sick, but almost unreal – I went to my work, and during the coffee-break with the residents, the coordinating charge nurse entered with the words: "Well, that wasn't a very good evening, was it?". I felt no need to make a serious response. My reaction was: "No, I have certainly had more pleasant evenings than that", to which there was no response at all. The department psychiatrist showed no interest. A few days later, however, I got a real telling-off from the department concerned. I phoned them, but no one answered and no one showed any interest. The whole affair was being evaluated, and my first thought was "shouldn't I be there then?". Apparently not. The same coordinating charge nurse came to me with the question of what we should do if the wife of the man who had thrown himself in front of the train asked to see him. She has a right to that, after all. As far as I was concerned, the charge nurse would have to solve that problem himself. I had no more energy for it.

I fail to understand how something like this can happen in psychiatry. One might have thought that it is precisely in psychiatry that one could expect to find the necessary expertise on what can go wrong in an individual's life. Certainly when one unexpectedly finds oneself in a situation like this. I am convinced that an outsider would not be able to understand what was going on here. It seems that from time to time, even in the field of psychiatry, that there is no real understanding. The support offered to me was *zero*, despite the fact that we often talk about empathy. I shall, of course, never be able to forget it all, but there is also no forgiveness for the shortcomings.'

In many health institutions, there are few, if any, support provisions for personnel confronted by disturbing incidents. Most organizations have not developed any policies for these situations. This is partly due to the suppressed belief that within these institutions nurses are trained to help others and that, armed with this knowledge and skill, they should be capable of helping both themselves and their colleagues: 'They will help each other whenever necessary'. After all, we don't need to teach farmers how to milk their cows, and by the same token giving help in times of suffering and setbacks is the very essence of the nursing profession. The failure to provide this kind of personnel care is sometimes justified on the basis of work-pressure or staff shortages. Another explanation is that nurses are expected to be able to withstand disturbing incidents: 'otherwise, they are not suitable for the job'.

Those unable to take stress leave, and the 'real' nurses will remain. The nursing profession loses many very good nurses in this way, every year.

It is too optimistic to think that nurses caught in these situations will themselves send out an SOS if they find themselves in psychological difficulties following a shock event. Studies have shown that it is precisely those who are in a really bad way who make no requests for help. Many nurses and assistant nurses are afraid to air their feelings: 'they will think I am a failure or a softy'. Or 'If I tell my (senior)colleagues what is on my mind, they will think I am a poor nurse'. The most important reason, however, why nurses will not talk about disturbing events they have experienced, is that they are shocked by their own emotions. They don't recognize themselves. It is very human to want to try to come clean with themselves before involving others. Unfortunately, however, the longer it takes to get themselves more or less back on course, the more difficult it becomes to reveal their true feelings.

And because many nurses hide their feelings, it is very difficult for senior (colleagues) to help them. They often notice that someone is behaving differently, but do not connect it with a shock event of some kind. They assume that the changed behaviour arises from problems in his or her private life, work-dissatisfaction, or for some other 'normal' reason.

In institutions where there is some degree of collegial support, the matter often rests at one or two talks. 'Then it should be over' or 'it will have passed by now'. The so-called *de-briefing* or initial talk, often lacks the necessary depth. Nurses very often only possess the art of actively listening – crucial in this kind of initial talk – to a very limited degree (indeed they cannot be blamed for it, many have simply not had the necessary training). In this chapter, we will look at what these institutions can do to create the best possible health situation for their own staff.

Information

Information is the primary and most important element in giving support and help. Information provision implies that all personnel employed in a health organization should be informed about human reactions to (psycho)traumas and how people come to terms with them. This information should include the elements described in Chapter 2. It is recommended that nursing staff be informed both verbally and in writing. This might be by means of a printed brochure giving basic information on shock events and how to deal with their after-effects. A letter could be included with this brochure indicating that at a specified date the subject will be discussed further within the department. This brochure should be sent to the home addresses of the staff; the advantage of this is that others on the home-front will probably see it and it will be discussed within the home atmosphere. This should not be under-estimated because it is usually the parent(s), partner, children and others close to the person concerned who are the people most directly confronted by the consequences of a shock event. If they know what a psychotrauma entails, they are likely to be more understanding in their reactions to it, and in this context will often be the most important people in spotting the signs and in provid-ing the necessary sympathy and support.

It is also recommended that the brochure be routinely distrib-uted during a nurse's introductory period, because practice has shown that it is during the early periods on the ward that the risks of a psychotrauma are greatest. New personnel also includes student nurses working for short training periods on the wards; and perhaps no group of nurses is more vulnerable than these.

The establishment of a support team

The second step in an institution's provision of care for its own personnel is the establishment of support teams: nurses who, following any shock incident, be it large or small, give support by talking in detail with the colleague(s) concerned. It is very difficult to be able to give a general picture of how health institutions should set up this kind of staff-support mechanism. In a small institution, with less than 150 personnel, for instance, everyone generally knows everyone else, but this is of course impossible in institutions employing 5000 people. The size of an institution's staff structure obviously determines how the kind of support we are talking about is given. In every case, however, what really matters is that people at the workface, as it were, are involved as much as possible in the selection and composition of a support system. One can, for instance, start by an open candidacy, i.e. any one can apply, as is done when Staff Council elections are held. The selection committee can comprise: boardroom representation, managerial representation, a staff council member, the personnel manager, the head of the nursing staff, an internal psychologist (or social worker), or an external expert with a psychological back-ground. The most important selection criterion is that the 'sup-porter' enjoys the trust of the nursing staff. He or she should be 'well liked' within a team or department. The trust will often decrease the central, or leadership, role the person in question plays in an organization. It will be difficult for those concerned in the shock events to discuss problems with someone on whom he or she is dependent and who can damage his or her career chances.

Another criterion, often closely connected with the above, is that the supporter must possess a considerable degree of social skills. It is not necessary that he or she is trained in all discussion principles and techniques. Such people are, alas, in very short supply, even in the nursing profession. What is more important is that he or she should have the capacity to become adept at applying these principles. No candidate-supporter can, or should, be expected to hold the necessary support-talks without proper and prior training. A short and practical training course (6–8 2-hour sessions) will be required if they are to gain the necessary skills.

A third selection criterion for would-be supporters is that they themselves are not suffering from a post-traumatic stress syndrome. If someone is still preoccupied with the consequences of a shock event in his or her own life, the chances are high that he or she will be completely overwhelmed by the confrontation with some-one else's suffering. This can lead to his or her, under the pretext of sharing experiences, bringing his or her own emotions so much to the forefront, that the other person hardly enters the picture at all.

A fourth criterion is that the supporter should have had a reasonable degree of work experience. Someone young and new, who has hardly had a chance to learn the tricks of the trade, will find it very difficult to win the confidence of other colleagues: 'she has only just arrived, how can she help me?' Another aspect is that junior nurses run more risks themselves of becoming traumatized in the wake of a disturbing incident.

A fifth, and last, criterion is the need for a large degree of 'availability'; the candidate-supporter must be prepared to give 'acte de présence', whenever the need arises and whenever called upon to do so – even outside working hours. (The extra time given to this support work must of course be compensated.)

The content of the training is divided into two parts. The future 'supporter' must possess elementary theoretical knowledge about trauma and trauma-coping (as described in Chapters 2 and 3). Even more important is that he/she also becomes proficient in the most essential communication and counselling skills.

Once a support team has been selected and trained, decisions will have to be made on the question of the team's authority. The following matters will have to be regulated:

o when will the supporter be called in?

o to which other professionals can the supporter turn for counsel if he himself has questions or problems?

o financial compensation or who will take over the supporter's duty periods?

When to call in the support team

Support and spotting is primarily the responsibility of the nursing team itself, with senior staff playing in important part in this. Particularly in the case of smaller incidents – and most incidents fall within this category – the team's task will be to provide colleague support in difficult situations.

'I was working as a nurse on the children's ward of a general hospital. I was nursing a child who did not appear to be particularly ill at first, but became increasingly ill as the day progressed. Her condition became so bad that she had to be transferred to a teaching hospital, and I accompanied her in the ambulance. When we arrived at the hospital, her condition had become even more critical – and she died there that same night. In the days that followed I experienced no 'support' from either the paediatrician or the charge nurse. This experience has always remained with me, and I would like to see support for anyone in this kind of situation.'

It is all too easy, and basically incorrect, to place these cases immediately in the hands of a support team member. The support-team should preferably only be called in for serious cases. A condition for support within one's own team is that there should be a climate in which it is considered quite normal for nurses to be emotionally 'hit' by situations they meet in their work. Unit or departmental discussions around a brochure on traumatic events, can be very fruitful here.

If a whole team, or a large part of it, is involved in a shock event, a member of the support team should be called in. This can lead the way to the formation of a self-help or fellow-sufferer group. In the case, too, of a serious incident which makes a very great impact on the team itself, or if someone reacts with extreme emotion to an event and/or that emotional reaction is difficult to comprehend, it is usually advisable to call in someone from the support team.

In some situations, the nurse concerned and a charge nurse, for instance, don't really hit if off together, in which case the nurse is unable to unload her story because she does not feel entirely safe with her senior colleague. In cases like this, minor though they may be, someone from the support team should be contacted immediately. Also, when the nurse concerned does have a good relationship with her senior colleague, but is afraid to unload her story for fear of being judged negatively (e.g. 'unable to take stress'), the nurse should be afforded the possibility of immediately approaching the support team herself.

There is no argument whatsoever among the experts as to when the support should start: as soon as possible. Anyone experiencing a shock event of some kind should preferably have his/her first support-talk within 24 hours. Everything possible should be done to ensure that the nurse can relate what has happened, and how he/she felt/feels about it, before he/she goes home that day; and there must be no exceptions to this golden rule, even if the incident occurs at the end of the duty period. There will, however, be situations in which the initial support is too little or too late, and for various reasons: the nurse, for whatever reason, has failed to report the incident, or he/she has talked about it but his/her colleagues have merely listened, unaware of its full significance, or serious but flawed or insufficient attention has been given to the matter. In these cases, the nurse concerned – certainly if she is also unable to unload her story at home – may develop physical and psychological disorders later.

If a nurse behaves differently from her normal pattern, those around her should seriously consider the possibility of it being linked to an earlier shock event. Those who are aware of the behaviour change – such as (senior) colleagues, personnel consultants – can make approaches to the nurse concerned and subtly inquire if there is something troubling her. If it does transpire that the behaviour change is indeed connected to an earlier disturbing event she has experienced, it is worth considering the possibility of contacting a member of the support team. Referral to a supporter is also the proper thing to do if the supportive efforts of the team in which the nurse works, are not having the desired effect. In order for nurses to be able to call in the help of the support team at any time, every member of the organization should be supplied with a list of the names and address of all the supporters.

Supporting the support team

Despite good information and training, the supporters themselves will also need support from time to time. They will be confronted in practice with situations for which they are not prepared. For their peace of mind and to ensure effective support, it is important that they too have access to external consultants who can help them with their difficulties and questions. The main question initially will be: 'Am I doing it right?' In the event of an institution having its own psychologist or psychiatrist – and this is usually the case in the larger institutions – it is obvious that their services should also be available to the supporter, on the understanding of course that they have the necessary expertise in treating psycho-traumas. If there is no internal staff member available for consult-ation, the institution should investigate whether a similar institution in the area has a psychologist or psychiatrist available for the task. Contacts can also be made, of course, with the local Mental Health Care Centre.

There should, in any case, be clear agreements on which professionals can be consulted. And there must also be clear guidelines on the extent to which supporters can themselves refer their 'clients' to the professionals if the difficulties become too great for the support team to carry.

Formal aspects

A condition for the adequate functioning of a support team is that the formal aspects are properly regulated beforehand. Compensa-tion, for instance – in money or compensatory hours – for the supporter called in outside working hours. Or compensation for the team of which the supporter is a member which – in normal working hours – is called upon to help another team. In order to avoid problems in retrospect, the supporter's appointment must be confirmed by one of the line-executives holding a central position in the organization, such as a personnel consultant, care manager, division manager or deputy director.

Finally, a warning: an organization needs to be absolutely clear on the purpose of a support team. One of the dangers is that the support team becomes to be regarded as a kind of 'complaints bureau' or (alternative) staff council: whenever members feel they have been treated badly or discourteously by one or more of their colleagues, or that things are not going well in a department or team, they make approaches to the support team in the hope that they will be able to take the matter on. This is, however, not the purpose for which the support team has been established.

Experience with self-help teams within police organizations has taught us that a support team undermines its own position when it complies with requests to defend the interests of people on the work-floor. If they do, then it very soon means that not only is the support team unable to cope with the workload, but that they will also lose the trust of the line executives who will then make no further referrals to them. Even though people may well like support teams to do more than they we were established to do, they should nonetheless realize that supporters lack the authority and the canals through which they can exert any influence. In short: it will end up with all parties being disappointed if the support team exceeds its mandate. What the support team can, and should, do is to spot where, and in which situations, nurses run a greater risk of shock-event confrontations than elsewhere, and how the conditions within a team can be improved.

As long as they concentrate on trauma support and the prevention of shock events, the support team will be regarded as an equal discussion partner, worthy of being taken seriously.

The initial support talk

As has already been stated, the support should be given as soon as possible after the disturbing incident has occurred. During the initial support talk, the nurse concerned is invited to relate what has happened as comprehensively as possible. Following the first broad description of the event, the nurse will be asked to re-run the film, as it were, in slow-motion, with the intention of becoming informed not only about the images but also about the impressions made on the other senses. One question, in particular, should always be asked: 'what has made the deepest impression on you?', or even more concrete: 'what (which image) has remained most clearly in your mind?' A healthy coming-to-terms-process is thereby set in motion. If the discussions take place in groups because several people have been involved in the incident in question, the supporter will have to ensure that everyone in turn is given an opportunity to express his/her feelings on the subject. The supporter must also emphasize the fact that everyone has his/her own story to tell and that no one's story is better (or worse) than the other. Each person can experience the event differently, and it should be stated prior to the onset of the discussion that all information will be treated as strictly confidential. In order to guarantee this, it is important that the discussions take place in a quiet environment, open to as few interruptions as possible.

During the initial support-talk, the nurse concerned should always be encouraged to discuss the event at home. Nothing is more difficult for a partner or children than silence – they are nearly always the ones to know that something is wrong. Uncertainty creates far more torment than the truth, even though the truth may be painful. Openness will enable the home-front to offer support. The initial support talk should also include a discussion on the type of emotional and physical reactions which can be expected in the wake of a disturbing incident. This should even be discussed in institutions or organizations which have issued the necessary information material. People in a crisis situation often forget the simplest things and doubt their own knowledge.

Practical issues should also be dealt with during the initial support-talk, such as: the legal aspects of a nursing error. And, if relevant, these matters should be handled during or after the initial talk, if possible in consultation with the nurse's immediate senior colleague or someone else holding a key position in the organization.

At a later stage, it is always wise to enquire about reactions within the nurse's immediate environment. It often appears that relatives and friends are unable to respond adequately, and this is also true of colleagues. The supporter can then explain that there is usually nothing sinister behind these reactions, but that they usually occur because of ignorance or a feeling of being ill-equipped to help. They want to help or give comfort, but don't know how. In order to avoid disappointments of this kind, the nurse concerned should be warned in the first support talk that not everyone will respond with the same degree of sympathy or understanding.

The number of talks required will depend on the seriousness of the incident and the degree of its emotional impact on those concerned. A minimum of two talks will certainly be required, whilst in serious cases ten talks, or even more, will be needed. The stress reactions will usually lessen in the course of time. If, however, there has been no visible improvement within the first two months, then we are dealing with a coping disorder and the supporter will have to refer the nurse for further professional help. After two months, even if only two support talks were necessary, the supporter should inquire of the nurse how things are going with her. This is because, in some cases, the real reaction becomes evident some time later, or there may even be a relapse.

References

Bergsma, A. (1994) 'Het gezicht als gesloten of open boek' (The face as an open or closed book). In *Psychologie (Psychology)*, March.

Borghstijn, M. and Johannes, W. (1992) 'Nee, daar kom ik niet voor' (No that is not what I have come for). In *Thuiszorg (Home Care)*, October.

Bout, J. van den and Kleber, R. (1994) *Omgaan met verlies en geweld (Coping with loss and violence)*. Utrecht: Kosmos/Zomer & Kreuning.

Bijl, R. and Lemmens, F. (1993) *Aan het werk. Een verkennend onderzoek naar gezondheidsrisico's van werkers in de geestelijke gezondheidszorg (Working. An exploratory study into health risks among workers in mental health care)* Nederlands Centrum Geestelijke Volksgezondheid (Netherlands Mental Health Care Centre), Utrecht.

Buijssen, H. (1992) 'Emotioneel trauma van verpleegkundigen nog te vaak afgedaan als beroepsrisico' (Emotional trauma among nurses – still too often brushed aside as a job-hazard). In *Verpleegkunde Nieuws (Nursing News) 40*, 14–17.

Buijssen, H.P.J. (1995) Burn-out voorkomen met trauma-opvang (Burn-out prevention by means of trauma-support). *Leeftijd (Age)* 7/8, 4–5.

Carmel, H. and Hunter, M. (1989) 'Staff injuries from in-patient violence.' *Hospital and Community Psychiatry 40*, 1, 41–45.

Davidowitz, M. and Myrick, R.D. (1984) 'Responding to the bereaved: an analysis of "helping" statements.' In *Research Record*, 1, 35–42.

Dekker, J. and Iping, J. (1995) Agressie in de psychiatrie (Agression in Psychiatry). *Gedrag en gezondheid (Behaviour and Health) 23*, 1, 30–34,

Herman, J.L. (1992) *Trauma and recovery*. New York: Basic Books.

Ignatieff, M. (1993) *Scarred Tissue*. London: Chatto and Windus.

McMillan, I. (1993a) 'A disturbing picture'. *Nursing Times 89*, 8, 30–34.

McMillan, I. (1993b) 'Emotional turmoil.' *Nursing Times 89*, 8, 36–37.

O'Connor, N. (1984) Letting go with love. The grieving process. La-Mariposa Press,Arizona.

Ravenscraft, R. (1994) 'After the crisis.' *Nursing Times 90*, 12, 26–28.

Roth, P. (1993) *Operation Shylock. A confession.* London: Cape.

Ryan, J. and Poster, E. (1993) 'Work place violence.' *Nursing Times 89*, 48, 38–41.

Scott, M.J. and Stradling, G.S. (1994) *Counselling for Post-Traumatic Stress Disorder.* London: Sage.

Velde, P.G. van der and Herpers, T.M.M. (1994) Agressie door psychiatrische patienten (Aggression by psychiatric patients). *Gedrag en Gezondheid (Behaviour and Health) 23*, 1, 29–33.

Vinton, L. and Mazza, N. (1994) 'Aggressive behaviour directed at nursing home personnel by residents' family members'. *The Gerontologist 34*, 4, 528–533.

Visser, G. (1994) *In gesprek met Jan Wouters (Talking with Jan Wouters).* Amsterdam: 5*8 Paperbacks.

About the author

Huub Buyssen (1953) studied Psychology in Nijmegen, his specialization being psycho-gerontology. For some years he worked part-time in the Social Gerontology Institute at the University of Nijmegen and as psychotherapist. He later worked for eleven years as a psycho-gerontologist in a city home care centre, and since 1 January 1995 has been working as a clinical psychologist in the W.A. Hoeve psychiatric hospital, which is part of the Rümke Group, in Den Dolder/Utrecht, The Netherlands.

Request:

The author would very much like to come into contact with nurses and assistant nurses who have experienced any kind of shock event in their work, and who would like to give a written report on it. It may be possible to include these – anonymously, if desired – in a subsequent edition of this book. The author is also open to reactions to – or critical commentary on – the contents of this present book.

All communications should be addressed to:

> Huub Buyssen
> H.C. Rümke Groep, Kruidenhof
> Dolderseweg 164
> 3734 BN Den Dolder
> The Netherlands